T0274960

Praise for *Silicon Heartland*

"No place or company is immune from getting disrupted—and Silicon Valley is no different. In Rebecca's new book, *Silicon Heartland*, she explores the tech innovation frontier emerging in states that were once centers of commerce but were left behind when they didn't adapt to new technologies."

—John Chambers, founder and CEO of JC2 Ventures and former executive chairman and CEO of Cisco Systems

"Rebecca Fannin's compassionate and rigorous analysis of entrepreneurship is a must-read. She asks and answers so many of the right questions: how we got here, where we're going, and what needs to happen to revitalize communities and democratize innovation. An indispensable book for founders, investors, and change-makers."

—Jim Breyer, founder and CEO, Breyer Capital

"In *Silicon Heartland*, Fannin details the technology transformation underway in our heartland—masterfully weaving together years of research and knowledge with personal stories from people across America. It's a book that inspires hope for our future."

—Ro Khanna, author of *Dignity in a Digital Age*

"Rebecca Fannin journeys back to her home in the Midwest to explore how cities and states are working to reinvent local economies. Her unique perspective will help readers understand the entrepreneurial communities that are working to turn cities between the coasts into promising innovation hubs."

—Steve Case, cofounder of AOL and Revolution and author of *The Rise of the Rest*

"*Silicon Heartland*, Rebecca Fannin's uplifting journey into America's all-too-often overlooked Midwest—where she herself grew up—is a compelling counter-narrative to the depiction of the region as being in the grip of post-industrial decline. This is the untold story of the Rust Belt rising, amid a wave of optimism, innovation, and old-fashioned grit."

—Maëlle Gavet, CEO of Techstars and author of
Trampled by Unicorns

"*Silicon Heartland* shines the light on exciting examples and best practices that are leveling the playing field of opportunity and unleashing new opportunity. This book is a must-read for anyone who believes that entrepreneurial success is only possible on the coasts. The Silicon Heartland welcomes you!"

—Brad D. Smith, president of Marshall University
and former chairman and CEO, Intuit

"*Silicon Heartland* provides an almost perfect sequel to Ms. Fannin's must-read *Tech Titans of China*. Now she brings the focus back to our nation's shores, but rather than detail the assumed decay of American greatness, she instead finds hope. A much-needed boost of optimism at a time when it's vitally needed."

—Chris Fenton, film producer and author of *Feeding the Dragon*

"An insightful look into the rebirth of cities and a region that launched American leadership in the global economy."

—Dan Schwartz, former publisher, *Asian Venture Capital Journal,*
and author, *The Future of Finance*

"*Silicon Heartland* is a fascinating and inspiring read. Only Rebecca Fannin, with her venture background, China experience, and heartland roots, could uncover the amazing tech revolution occurring in the middle of America."

—David Kaufman, director of global strategies, Nixon Peabody

"*Silicon Heartland* shows how scrappy innovators are remaking the US economy and breathing life back into Rust Belt cities and impoverished rural communities. Fannin does a fantastic job providing both the data and case studies on how a new wave of entrepreneurs and technology are transforming America's overlooked and underfunded regions."

—Steve Hoffman, chairman and CEO, Founders Space

"Finally . . . someone gets it. The Rust Belt of the Midwest is transitioning to the tech belt of the heartland, and Rebecca A. Fannin tells that story in an engaging and personal manner. A must-read for those who think the Rust Belt is dead and buried and a book that, while still being realistic about challenges, fills the reader with hope and promise."

—Tom Hodson, director emeritus of the E. W. Scripps School of Journalism and WOUB Public Media

"Few journalists I know have truly been 'out there,' deeply connecting with their subject like Rebecca. Her family's personal history in the Midwest allows her to truly hear what's happening."

—Brian Cohen, founding partner, NY Venture Partners, and chairman, Science Literacy Foundation

"From an author with America's heartland in her blood and a keen observer of global innovation, this book is a tremendous resource to help communities across the country tap into their entrepreneurial roots and reinvent themselves."

— Greg Becker, president and CEO of Silicon Valley Bank

Silicon Heartland

Silicon Heartland

Transforming the Midwest from Rust Belt to Tech Belt

Rebecca A. Fannin

Copyright © 2023 by Rebecca A. Fannin

All rights reserved, including the right of reproduction in whole or in part in any form. Charlesbridge and colophon are registered trademarks of Charlesbridge Publishing, Inc.

At the time of publication, all URLs printed in this book were accurate and active. Charlesbridge and the author are not responsible for the content or accessibility of any website.

An Imagine Book
Published by Charlesbridge
9 Galen Street
Watertown, MA 02472
(617) 926-0329
www.imaginebooks.net

Library of Congress Cataloging-in-Publication Data
Names: Fannin, Rebecca A., author.
Title: Silicon heartland: transforming the Midwest from rust belt to tech belt / by Rebecca A. Fannin.
Description: Watertown: Charlesbridge Publishing, [2023] | Includes bibliographical references. | Summary: "How the American Midwest is recovering its economic weight as a center for high tech and innovation."—Provided by publisher.
Identifiers: LCCN 2022000881 (print) | LCCN 2022000882 (ebook) | ISBN 9781623545567 (hardcover) | ISBN 9781632892508 (ebook)
Subjects: LCSH: High technology industries—Middle West. | Technological Innovations—Economic aspects—Middle West. | Economic Development—Middle West. | Middle West—Economic conditions—21st century.
Classification: LCC HC107.A14 F36 2022 (print) | LCC HC107.A14 (ebook) | DDC 330.977—dc23/eng/20220422
LC record available at https://lccn.loc.gov/2022000881
LC ebook record available at https://lccn.loc.gov/2022000882

Display type set in Agenda by Greg Thompson and Cheap Pine by Hannes von Döhren from HVD Fonts
Text type set in ITC Galliard by Matthew Carter
Wheat photo by Hamza Madrid on Unsplash
Printed by Maple Press in York, Pennsylvania
Production supervision by Jennifer Most Delaney
Jacket design by Nicole Turner
Interior design by Mira Kennedy

Printed in the United States of America
(hc) 10 9 8 7 6 5 4 3 2 1

Photographs on pages vi and 155 courtesy of the author

To my mom and dad who taught me the values of the heartland
  and
my siblings who keep me grounded with traditions
  and
my husband, John, who showed me a world of contrasts in New York
  and
innovators everywhere who continue to inspire me

Contents

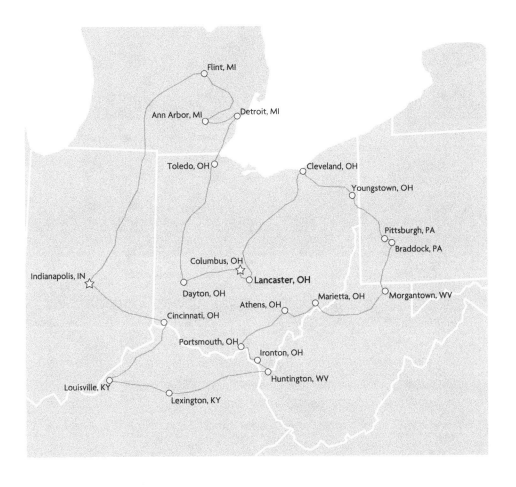

Silicon Heartland tracks my journey through the American Midwest as I became a witness to what I see as a great American industrial revival. What is known as the Rust Belt stretches across eight states, from central New York to southeast Wisconsin, concentrated mostly around the Great Lakes, and its twenty-six Rust Belt cities having a combined population of 7.8 million. Overlapping the Rust Belt is Appalachia, which tracks the Appalachian Mountains and runs across twelve states, from northern Mississippi to southern New York, and has a population of 25.7 million. My trip focused on Michigan, Indiana, and four states in Central Appalachia: Kentucky, Ohio, Pennsylvania, and West Virginia.

Introduction

In the summer of 2019, a front-page headline in the *New York Times* caught my attention. "Opioid Overdoses Reach Second Highest in the Nation." The dateline was Minford, Ohio—the rural town in southeastern Ohio where my parents grew up and met in high school. It's near where my relatives still reside on farms passed down through generations, since the time when my ancestors, the Gampps, came to the United States from Germany in the 1830s. The article chronicled despair, hopelessness, jobs, and poverty. My family's country. As I flipped through the newspaper, I found myself quoted as an expert on China's rivalry with Silicon Valley.

The contrast between the American heartland and the coasts is something I know about. After graduating from Ohio University, I left the foothills of Appalachia for Manhattan. My career began in a cubicle at Crain Communications, where I scored some front-page articles and even had my own column. During the late-nineties dotcom boom, I covered the internet bubble for the Silicon Valley magazine *Red Herring*—at least until it burst in 2001. Halfway around the world, tech innovation was emerging in Beijing and Shanghai. So I followed the trail and became one of the first American journalists to cover China's entrepreneurial boom. My first book, *Silicon Dragon*, was published in 2008, when no one was predicting that China could win a tech race. *Tech Titans of China*, eleven years later, proved I was right very early—but not without controversy. Television anchors grilled me about China's challenge to US innovation leadership. "Are they spying on us? Are they stealing from us?"

So change and innovation are something else I know about. Which is why I decided to investigate another pivotal transformation—this time in my homeland. Because that *Times* article told only half the story. Yes, America's industrial Midwest, the once-proud bastion of well-paying jobs and middle-class life, has come to evoke bleakness. As the *Times* article showed, the collapse of steel mills, chemical plants, and coal mines over the past fifty years devastated the region. And those blue-collar jobs aren't coming back. Automation, robotics, artificial intelligence, and offshoring production to China have seen to that.

But a new mind-set has emerged. An innovative mind-set. As John Chambers, the former CEO of Cisco Systems, put it, "When the factories and mines closed, our drive, dreams, and curiosity were lost. Now we need to dream again, and to achieve those dreams we need to become a startup country." His deeply ingrained lesson? "We need to stay ahead of market transitions, to disrupt or be disrupted."

That lesson has been heeded. What has been known as the Rust Belt—a symbolic name for the rusting out of idled steel mills and auto factories—is now shedding its rust and developing the shine of a Tech Belt. This former pinnacle of the US economy is making a comeback, which bodes well not just for our country's heartland but for our economy and morale nationwide. It's in sync with President Joe Biden's vow to "Build Back Better": to create millions of jobs, invest more in research and development and emerging technologies, and upgrade worker skills across a broad swath of America.

This renewal promises to rebalance the money and power that shifted to Silicon Valley—and to China. The Silicon Valley elite may have ridiculed the Midwest as "flyover country," but the heartland has begun the road to recovery. Yet it's a long road. The erosion of manufacturing work over the past decades can't be replaced by minimum-wage jobs. Many inner cities and rural towns in Middle America continue to struggle with population decline, poverty, opioid addiction, weak or no broadband, poor social services, crumbling infrastructure, and a diminishing tax base. Trashed eyesores remain.

Despite these very real obstacles, the revitalization of bygone industrial regions built on coal, iron ore, and oil by legends named Carnegie, Mellon, Rockefeller, and Frick is underway. Now, with more investment in startups, technologies, workforce retraining, infrastructure rebuilding, and R&D, the economic woes underlying Mid-American gloom are being reversed and helping us maintain our global innovative edge.

Tick Ridge Roots

My connection to the heartland is deep. One of four siblings, I grew up in an academic family in the foothills of the Appalachians. Our family has been here for seven generations, going back to the Gampps. My parents bettered themselves through a lifelong pursuit of learning, earning master's and doctoral degrees. A history professor at Ohio University, my father was always deep in his books. My mother earned extra credit as a kindergarten teacher, a disciplinarian who kept unruly five-year-olds in check on the playground and the classroom in morning and afternoon periods. After-school hours at our home were spent on homework—no TV watching, except *Captain Kangaroo* weekday mornings and *Lassie* on Sunday evening. Every summer my parents, older sister, two younger brothers, and I crammed into a classic VW camper microbus we'd nicknamed Mikey. We traveled for weeks at a time, from Ohio to Alaska to Mexico, and flew to European capitals and the former USSR. I loved exploring historic sites across North America, with my dad narrating and my mom navigating. We camped out in just about all the national parks. It was a childhood that broadened my horizons.

When I left my hometown of Lancaster, Ohio, years ago, I missed my family, but I also escaped the decline of smokestack cities and mining towns. I was the first in my extended family to leave the Buckeye State and one of very few in my high school graduating class to depart. Most got married, had kids, worked locally, and were part of the community. My former classmates remember me as a shy girl who embarrassed easily and played the flute, so they are puzzled by my distant ventures. And the siblings and cousins I played hide-and-seek with in the hayloft of my grandparents' barn in Scioto County aren't sure what to make of the lifestyle choices I've made.

At age thirty, I bought a riverfront co-op apartment in the 1911-built Riviera building in Manhattan's Washington Heights neighborhood. By the time I was thirty-seven, I was married to a New York City lawyer and was immersed in a roller-coaster editorial career in the center of trends, from media's transition from print to digital, to the Japanese buying spree of US real estate, to the developing markets of Eastern Europe, to the economic rise of China, and eventually to the decentralization of Silicon Valley. By venturing out, I escaped the Midwest's economic downturn, and a whole new world opened up. By the 1990s, I was editor-in-chief of *International Business* magazine and, later, an editor at *Ad Age International.* By 2000, I was immersed in digital publishing at *Red Herring.* Transitioning to a laptop and mobile phone, I wrote and edited articles entirely online for the first time. I could work from anywhere, and my traveling journalist days were launched. I was broadening my horizons again.

On the Road Again

But my travels were interrupted, as everyone's were, by the coronavirus pandemic. In early spring 2020, my overseas adventures ended. By then, I'd been running a media and events startup, Silicon Dragon Ventures, for ten years, focusing on emerging Silicon Valleys, particularly in China. It was time for something different. As I sheltered in place, I thought about a new editorial project I'd started the year before and now put it on fast-forward. Leveraging my more versatile schedule, I embarked on a heartland journey to uncover and chronicle stories of my homeland's left-behind manufacturing and coal-mining lands.

I went in search of what I instinctively sensed was a good news story brewing in my own backyard. *Silicon Heartland* is the product of that search—my discovery of how dozens of game-changers have set the stage for a great American turnaround, from the Appalachians in the east to the Rockies in the west.

The "flyover country" stereotype has existed for years. The Midwest has been seen as the home of manufacturing and mining dinosaurs. Of boring plodders. But these perceptions are outdated. Driving my Honda Element SUV—the closest match to the VW van of my childhood—I started a grassroots reporting journey. After a couple of probing journeys in 2019, I traveled most of summer 2020 and returned three more times over several months in 2021. It was a hands-on way of learning about the current state of the country. It was also a significant personal trip. Since graduating from Ohio University, I hadn't been back much. There had been little reason to go home, other than for holidays and funerals.

Home is the town of Lancaster in Fairfield County, just north of the Appalachian foothills. It was a good place to start and a great centralized base for traveling throughout the heartland, from the hollows of West Virginia to the rivers Allegheny, Monongahela, and Scioto; to the factory towns of Pittsburgh and Youngstown; to the motor cities of Detroit and Flint; to Hoosier country and the bluegrass of Kentucky. Google Maps on my smartphone was an able navigator. It was a trip down memory lane: I revisited the places of my childhood and the original homestead of my father's family on Kentucky's Zion Ridge, where there is still no running water and few paved roads, but a tobacco barn, a pond, cows, and mountain scenery. It was moving.

But I also brought my reporter's eye. As I explored these rustic spots decimated by industrial decline, I knew that innovation springs from necessity, from the worst of circumstances. And my onsite reporting of emerging economies throughout Asia helped me to recognize a developing region, this time in the American heartland. I put eight thousand miles on my Honda Element, driving on winding country roads past cornfields and pastures, and on flat interstate highways with billboards and mileage posts signaling my next destination. It's good that gasoline was cheap then.

Right here in Middle America, I discovered a reenergized economy built on optimism, innovation, sheer grit, and a strong work ethic. Throughout remote zip codes of Ohio, Michigan, Indiana, and Pennsylvania, I found aging, one-industry towns beginning to diversify. In previously forlorn places I discovered technologically advanced upstarts in biotech, 3D printing, self-driving cars, green energy, artificial intelligence, and robotics. I found all-American, higher-skilled (and higher-paying) jobs in a number of metro areas. I saw Zoom towns of remote worker-bees that had popped up in Appalachia. It was a trend that wouldn't have seemed obvious except that I took the time to explore, not just drive by on the freeway.

On my trip, I interviewed countless innovators who are digging out from the shutdown of auto- and steelmakers, mines, and chemical plants. There was space robotics technology in Pittsburgh searching for water on the moon; brain stimulation research in West Virginia seeking to cure Alzheimer's disease; and from Athens, Ohio, ultracold storage techniques for distributing vaccines to fight COVID.

My grand heartland journey started that hot summer of 2020. And while I conducted a few interviews over Zoom, most people were available for in-person meetings since no one was traveling. Of course, we were all wearing masks and social distancing. I met loads of scrappy entrepreneurs with big dreams, investors, town champions, mayors, coaches, mentors, and academics—more than 150 change-makers in all.

It was good to be back in the Appalachian foothills. At a red light in Zanesville, Ohio, once the pottery capital of the world, I asked a motorcyclist revving his motor in the next lane how to get to the Zane Grey Museum, which memorializes the building of the old National Road and the opening of the American Midwest. He shouted a rhythmic reply, "You go right on up that big, daammn hill." I understood. It was a pleasure to speak with locals and hear the familiar accents. Before they finished a sentence, I knew what they meant. Midwesterners still answer their phones. You get straight talk, albeit with some colloquialisms thrown in every now and then—chickens with their head cut off, cart before the horse, and so on.

Thirty miles southwest from Zanesville, past rich farmland on Route 22, is my hometown of Lancaster, the quintessential, all-American small town with a well-preserved historic square, museums and churches, a ten-day festival of arts and music held each July, and a sprawling fairgrounds dating from 1850, where you can still attend concerts, demolition derbies, tractor pulls, and the annual fair in October.

As teens, my sister and I complained that there was nothing to do in town, if you didn't count the drive-in movie theater or the Tiki swimming pool and bowling alley with their tropical, thatched-hut themes. My father would respond that Lancaster, with its family-friendly values, was a good place to raise kids. It was also a step up from our prior home in Jackson, a smaller, rural town of 6,000, sixty-five miles south, that was once known for rich iron resources but best remembered for its annual apple festival and parade, foot-long hot dogs, and homemade ice cream. My dad ran a Nationwide Insurance agency in Jackson and drove a VW bug. But at age forty-three, he found his calling as a history professor at Ohio University's newly opened Lancaster campus.

Lancaster has some national history to it. It was home to Civil War general William Tecumseh Sherman and his younger brother Senator John Sherman (of the Sherman Anti-Trust Act of 1890), as well as Senator and Secretary of the Treasury Thomas Ewing, and Secretary of the Interior and US Attorney General Henry Stanbery. Their residences are among several well-preserved historic houses in the center of town. For yearbook memories, my high school lockermate was Miss Teenage America Colleen Fitzpatrick, now an actress. A cheerleading classmate was the younger sister of globally acclaimed artist Jenny Holzer, known for her truisms, or holzer grams, which reflect the "tell it like it is" culture I grew up in. With my all-American upbringing and trademark long, straight, dirty blonde hair and bright, flowery clothes, it's no wonder that my editors in New York City would kiddingly sing to me Leonard Bernstein's song from the 1953 musical *Wonderful Town*: "Why, Oh Why, Oh Why, Oh Why Did I Ever Leave Ohio."

Lancaster is a quintessential heartland city. And like all flyover towns, it suffered major blows from the decline of its manufacturing stronghold. In 1984, the town's largest employer, the glassware maker Anchor Hocking, shut one of its plants. Its once-5,000-strong workforce was eventually reduced to 800, shattered due to lower-cost production in China and Mexico, a fiscal crisis, and mismanagement by Wall Street financiers. The same year, Kresge's five-and-dime store and Hickle's department store closed. In 2007, Lancaster Glass shut down a century-old plant and left 140 laborers out of work.

And yet, as I learned when I revisited, it's coming back. This town of 40,000, with a growing population, is a satellite of booming Columbus and a good example of the heartland revitalization I had come to explore. Prices of newly constructed houses and apartments in Lancaster are rising 10 percent or more a year, and Google recently bought 120 acres to build a data center here. It's on the move.

One of my first stops after my hometown was Dayton, a hundred miles west of Lancaster, a city famous for its influential inventions, including the airplane, the cash register, the self-starting auto ignition, and the pop-up top to open cans. The city brought back memories of my college internship at the *Dayton Journal Herald*. I couldn't wait to see the newsroom, the printing presses, and the bar next door where we chilled out each night, waiting for the first print editions. But the bar has been torn down. And the ornate, four-story headquarters where I had written headlines and edited newswire copy had been vacant since 2007 and was now surrounded by parking lots and the remains of razed buildings.

Yet I could see that the city's entrepreneurial spirit lives on. Tech startups have moved into rehabbed warehouses and restored complexes downtown. Founders are feeding off of technology licensed from the Air Force Research Laboratory in Dayton to launch high tech businesses. In the southernmost Ohio River town of Ironton, not far from where I was born, a plastics waste recycling facility has broken ground on the site of a former Dow Chemical factory, relying on Procter & Gamble patents that promise to save the planet.

From Flyover to Fly-in

Without fanfare, a pivotal movement has been growing to restore the American dream in towns like Lancaster and cities like Dayton. Tech ecosystems—entrepreneurial talent, accelerators, incubators, universities, and scientific breakthroughs—are retooling midsized heartland cities and Appalachian towns. Remote regions that were nearly forgotten when the money and power shifted to Silicon Valley—and to China—are being rebooted. Who doesn't want to be part of a reemerging American frontier that's bringing back jobs, raising incomes, and helping us beat back China?

It's true that the Midwest doesn't yet boast a high-profile tech company like Apple or Tesla or Zoom (though Intel has announced a $20 billion investment in central Ohio). Nor does it have a venture capital player in the league of Sequoia Capital or Accel or Andreessen Horowitz. But Pittsburgh, Youngstown, Cleveland, Detroit, and other cities that defined yesterday's industrial revolution are evolving as high-tech centers.

Prominent Silicon Valley leaders such as Salesforce and Oracle are swooping in to acquire cutting-edge companies in the Midwest. Tech icons like Cisco's John Chambers and Brad Smith, previously with Intuit, are creating entrepreneurial sparks in Appalachia with philanthropic and funding efforts to revitalize the poverty-stricken state. Chambers helped convince Richard Branson to locate a center for the futuristic high-speed transit tube Hyperloop on the site of a former coal mine in West Virginia. The venture firm Drive Capital, launched in Columbus by two former Sequoia Capital partners from the Bay Area, is bringing Silicon Valley–style investing to Middle America and has already backed more than sixty startups regionwide, with several wins, including tech-powered auto insurer Root and language-learning app Duolingo.

As Drive Capital's cofounder Mark Kvamme told me over lunch in the hip Short North district of Columbus, "You don't have to be in Silicon Valley to build a great technology company."

With so much at stake in revitalizing the Rust Belt and bringing back jobs, it's no wonder that big names in business and politics are putting time, energy, and money into a turnaround. Billionaires like Steve Case and Michael Bloomberg are spearheading a drive, including actual bus tours, to open investor's eyes to an untapped entrepreneurial talent well in the Midwest. Representative Tim Ryan (D-Ohio) accompanied some of these venture tours. As he put it, "There's a valley of death for early startups that need money to scale up. These tours align capital with the opportunities they don't see in Silicon Valley."

These Rust Belt safaris reminded me that high tech and venture capital interest in China was fast-tracked after partners from Sand Hill Road firms went on group tours to explore the emerging country's budding entrepreneurship. They came back in awe and made billions investing early in high-growth Chinese startups that went public in New York, creating the Silicon Dragon, the Chinese tech-boom of the early 2000s.

Boomtowns Rising

Nearly three-quarters of venture capital investment continues to go to just three states: California, New York, and Massachusetts. But that's changing. As working remotely became common during the pandemic, Bay Area techies began relocating to midsized inland cities and the countryside,[1] where life is safer, less expensive, and more relaxed, with time for hiking, creek wading, and berry picking (my enjoyable pastimes in rural Ohio). Now that working from home and flexible schedules have emerged as not only viable but a trend, and Zoom meetings are the new normal, there's been a bit of a backlash against Silicon Valley as tech central. It's pricey, congested, and more and more affected by wildfires and droughts. Venture capitalists are looking elsewhere and finding small-scale, investable businesses in America's new frontier.

The Buckeye State I left years ago has emerged as a popular desti-nation in this migration to the nation's interior. Ohio's capital city, back in the day known as Cowtown, was where my relatives brought their produce and livestock to be exhibited and judged at the annual Ohio State Fair. Today Columbus, or Cbus as it's called, is booming with geeks, nerds, and millennials. Other previously neglected mid-western cities have been revitalized with cool, convenient neighbor-hoods and are attracting young, cosmopolitan professionals, reversing a brain drain of baby boomers like me who left a slumping economy for a brighter horizon.[2]

A massive cleanup is underway in polluted industrial cities that once ran on steel, iron ore, and coal. Giant steel and auto-making factories like Youngstown Sheet & Tube in northeastern Ohio and Buick City in Flint have gone under the wrecking ball. Rundown warehouses and closed department stores have been repurposed or torn down. In their place are data centers, coworking spaces, and high-ceiling lofts.

Construction zones are everywhere, similar to the building boom I saw in Shanghai and Beijing ten to twenty years ago. Columbus and

Indianapolis—cold winters aside—are rapidly expanding, with high-value jobs and civic amenities.[3] Rusting no more, Pittsburgh, Cleveland, Detroit, and Dayton are becoming tomorrow's boomtowns, no longer economic wastelands. (See table A.) And they need to be aggressive—they are competing with the Sun Belt states in the South and Southwest, which continue to beckon with warm climates, job opportunities, or in some cases, early retirement.[4]

The strategic tech adviser Peter Mullen packed his bags in 2021 and moved to Tulsa, the oil capital of the world which today is referred to as the Silicon Prairie. Taking advantage of remote working, the gig economy, as well as a $10,000 relocation incentive, he bought a new home for one-fifth the price of the Bay Area. Before even unpacking his bags, he was absorbed in the city's networking events for entrepreneurs. "It was a risk for me, but I'm thriving," he told me. Since launching in late 2018, the Tulsa Remote package has attracted 23,000 applicants and 900 new residents.

Could a *Shark Tank*-ization of Middle America really be possible? Will an Elon Musk be discovered in the Midwest? It's only a matter of time.

Building It Better

The Rust Belt's reboot coincides with governmental pledges to reenergize America's industrial economy with higher-skill jobs, rebuilt infrastructure, and additional investment in R&D. Manufacturing still accounts for 60 percent of our country's exports, but it has been hollowed out to less than 9 percent of the national workforce. Blue-collar factory work has declined from one-third of the country's employment in the 1950s to 8.5 percent today, while China has moved ahead as the world's largest producer.[5]

Yesterday's capitals of manufacturing—Cleveland, Pittsburgh, and Detroit—are rebuilding from economic hardships and aging infrastructure[6] that tore their core apart: 91,000 US factories were shuttered and five million manufacturing jobs were lost in two decades.[7] Outsourcing and a surge of China imports stripped away blue-collar labor at automakers, steel mills, iron foundries, and glassmakers. In a shift to natural gas and renewable energy sources, coal breakers closed in Appalachia and mining work plunged 41 percent from a high of 92,000 in 2011.[8]

Smokestack cities and coal country reflect the resulting sorrows: blocks of dilapidated homes, littered streets, vacant downtown retail shops, broken windows, empty factory shells, and pot-bellied beer drinkers hanging out on the front porch, cigarette in hand.

Now, potential is stirring as former manufacturing centers are being remade into innovation clusters that were inconceivable little more than a decade ago. In the past five years, some 640,700 tech jobs[9] have pumped up the $1.7 trillion technology market,[10] while nearly 32 million small businesses have accounted for two-thirds of new jobs since 2000.[11] Higher-skill, tech-driven smart factories could add 2.4 million jobs by 2030.[12] The engine of growth is high tech upstarts that are boosting innovation, productivity, and competitiveness, investing heavily in R&D, growing revenues, hiring knowledge workers, and paying good wages.[13]

The Mightier Middle

Several midwestern tech hubs are at the starting gate to be the next Silicon Valley, following the evolution of Silicon Beach in Los Angeles, Silicon Hills in Austin, and Silicon Alley in New York City, but each developing its own distinct identity. It's not about creating the next Pokémon Go or NFT. It's about practical technology applications in healthcare, finance, education, and transportation. Unlike fads that flamed out, mid-American tech is grounded in robotics, artificial intelligence, software services, green energy, 3D printing, and biotech. This force stands to transform the way we work, live, and play.

As the real estate saying goes, it's all about location, but it's also proximity to resources. Sand Hill Road, the nation's venture capital nucleus, sprang up right next to Stanford University. TusPark, Beijing's tech and venture hub, developed just outside the gates of Tsinghua University. Likewise, hubs in the Midwest leverage nearby talent, R&D, and intellectual capital. There's a tech buzz around such strongholds as the University of Michigan in Ann Arbor, the health-tech corridor around the world-renowned Cleveland Clinic, the 3D printing campus of the Youngstown Business Incubator, and Nationwide Insurance and Ohio State University in Columbus.

Pittsburgh's so-called Silicon Strip was once mainly warehouses. Today, it sports a newly built, four-story space for virtual reality labs creating avatars at Facebook (now Meta). Pittsburgh's remarkable high-tech climb from its Steel Town roots stems from engineering-strong Carnegie Mellon University. As former Pittsburgh mayor Bill Peduto has said, the city "still shows its scars from the past, but from fossil fuels and robotics, artificial intelligence, and biotech, we are building it better."

Of course, the Rust Belt's transformation hasn't reached everywhere. In some devastated, off-the-grid areas, change is glacial and largely anecdotal. Inexperience, lower expectations, capital shortages, and few advancement opportunities stand in the way. Newly empowered startups may fall short of replacing work lost due to deindustrialization. Marginalized people may not make it into the much-heralded middle class. But this push forward could narrow the stark economic divide between elite coastal states, with their gated communities, swimming pools, and Tesla cars, and the old Rust Belt, with its rusted-out factories; dilapidated trailer homes; and front yards full of junk cars, tires, and chickens.

The divide is still there. I saw it clearly as I drove along Route 50 through the mid-Ohio valley. Outside Parkersburg, I crossed a bridge spanning the Ohio River in view of chemical plants that had been in the news for legal battles over toxic contamination. Into the West Virginian Appalachians, across several hairpin turns in the mountains, I reached the once-thriving railroad town of Grafton, one of the state's poorest places, with few signs of commerce, a centuries-old station, and a hotel sitting vacant and in need of repair. Crossing the state line into northern Virginia, I saw a different world of the super-rich, an equestrian countryside fifty miles outside Washington, DC. Narrowing this divide may not happen in my lifetime, or longer.

Yet mid-American entrepreneurship stands a chance of bringing prosperity to more folks. To do so it needs to overcome a significant cultural barrier. The biggest limitation the Rust Belt faces is lack of confidence. Heartland entrepreneurs have technical talent to make new things, but when it comes to the big, visionary idea, well, that can be lacking. But, remember this frontier was once the innovation center of the world. The DNA of the Western Reserve pioneers is still there.

The Silicon Valley credo says take a risk and it's okay to fail (as long as you do another startup). But that doesn't translate well in the Midwest. Bragging may never be in style. In my San Francisco Bay neighborhood, people talk high tech, equity deals, venture capital, and startups at the local coffee shop. In the Ohio countryside, earning steady hourly pay and getting employee benefits can matter a lot more than a high from creating and running a startup. But as I've learned in the survival-of-the-fittest career boot camps of Manhattan and Silicon Valley, going bold matters.

Flown Over No More

Silicon Heartland offers an optimistic story of a region that has been overlooked and underestimated for too long by the urban elite. Each chapter tells the story of one part of my heartland journey. Taken together, these chapters paint a picture of resurgence in almost every economic and social category required to make this once-great region great again. This story introduces the resourceful people and behind-the-scene stories reinventing the American heartland. Hardscrabble American frontier folks, like the Chinese tech titans I reported on in my first book, are having a major impact on the retooling of the industrialized Midwest. The no-nonsense people of the Rust Belt know how to make things and get things done—even if they are sometimes faulted for not thinking big enough. My uncle Homer invented a yard maintenance tool that could be used as either an easy-to-operate, three-sided hedge clipper or a lawn mower. But he should have patented it.

The can-do people of mid-America, descendants of farmers and factory laborers, are surprising the coastal elites. With trademark resilience, grit, ingenuity, and hard work, heartland heroes and down-to-earth doers are transforming the Rust Belt into an emerging Tech Belt. As they do, I should have plenty more reason to come back home. It's time to change the script to *fly-in country*.

Table A: Top 15 Heartland Tech Markets on the Rise

	Tech Talent Pool	Percent Change, 5 years
Minneapolis	97,470	5.3%
Detroit*	89,680	4.5%
St. Louis	55,080	9.9%
Kansas City	52,630	8.0%
Columbus*	47,940	5.1%
Pittsburgh*	43,080	10.7%
Indianapolis*	39,990	23.2%
Cincinnati*	39,080	9.6%
Cleveland*	36,320	14.6%
Nashville	35,190	36.1%
Madison	24,580	31.9%
Omaha	22,600	17.0%
Louisville*	19,290	31.0%
Dayton*	18,930	31.0%
Tulsa	12,460	19.0%

Source: US Bureau of Labor Statistics, CBRE report, 2015–2020 data
* cities author toured for this book

PART ONE

The Innovators

Chapter One

The Scrappy Innovators

How inspiring entrepreneurs in Flint, Dayton, Indianapolis,
and Pittsburgh are helping to renew the heartland

In Like Flint

In the early 1970s, Flint, Michigan, had a population of 190,000 and General Motors employed 80,000 in surrounding Genesee County. In the ensuing decades, however, automation, poor car sales, and a shift to overseas production led to a sad downward spiral. Flint's population shrank to 81,000. More than one-third live in poverty,[14] one of the nation's highest rates.

Above the city's intersection of Saginaw and Detroit Streets, a wrought-iron arch still displays, in large lettering, "Flint Vehicle City." But these days, most people know Flint from its toxic water disaster, the subject of a 2017 documentary simply entitled *Flint,* which portrayed Middle America's crumbling infrastructure as a problem more characteristic of a third-world country than the first-world country we are. Or they know it from Michael Moore's 1989 documentary, *Roger & Me,* which examined the human impact of GM's closure of the Buick City complex and its layoffs of 30,000 workers at several Flint factories.

Yet the city is coming back, as I learned when I visited. I rose early one morning in Detroit and sped northwest on I-75, passing areas of urban blight ready for demolition—or repurposing. When I arrived, I discovered contrasting scenes: on one hand sagging, abandoned homes on weedy lots (a five-year city plan has demolished more than 5,000 blighted properties out of nearly 20,000 derelict homes, commercial structures, and vacant lots). On the other hand, I saw some beautifully renovated buildings, including the Capitol Theatre, reopened in 2017 after a $37 million, long-overdue restoration of the cinema and concert venue; the century-old Genesee County Savings Bank, which has been rehabilitated and transformed into a Hilton Garden Inn; and St. Paul's Episcopal Church, with its steeple towering over the heart of downtown.

I parked in a shady spot close to City Hall, where I admired the vintage red-brick streets dating back to 1898, the majestic county courthouse building, and a few blocks of well-kept downtown shops. The once-prosperous city didn't look so bad at street level.

That afternoon, I met Mayor Sheldon Neeley at City Hall. A lifelong resident of Flint and former local union president, city council member, and state representative, he was elected mayor in 2019, promising to unite and improve the city and fight blight. He candidly reflected about the city's "rough edges," an economic recovery "physically and psychologically," and in a play on words noted how "innovation is the child of necessity." He told me he is calling for $2 million in federal relief funds to be committed toward the effort to clean up the town's abandoned properties.

But I also wanted to get out there and meet some of the entrepreneurs who were helping Flint turn around already. I started with Detroit native Ali Rose VanOverbeke, whose eyeglass design company was near City Hall. After graduating from the Parsons School of Design, Ali Rose got a dream job as a fashion designer in Manhattan. But she wasn't fulfilled. On time out, she volunteered to teach sewing skills to domestic abuse victims in India and helped the Red Cross deliver cases of drinking water to Flint. In India, she saw the slums. In Flint, she found a shocking level of poverty. "It was worse here than what I had seen in India," Ali Rose recalled. "I had a personal calling to help Flint."

Back in the New York City grind after her volunteer experience, she couldn't help "thinking about Flint every day." She pondered how she could help rebuild the community using her design skills. With help from her professor, Jack Burns, she came up with the idea of starting a small business in Flint that neatly combines fashion, tech, sustainability, and social good.

"When I started, I wrote four goals on a Post-it note: reduce plastics, create a living wage job, give back to Flint, and encourage a circular economy," she said. She and I met at her coworking space in a recently opened innovation hub. Her startup's brand name is a riff on Genesee County, where Flint is located, and a play on what her startup does. Genusee designs eyeglass frames and makes them locally with a small group of workers who lost their jobs when the automakers shut down. The stylish frames are assembled from recycled plastic water bottles tossed out during the city's toxic water crisis.

When we met, Ali Rose, who is only thirty-two, was dressed in a bright yellow, flowing cotton dress and matching belt, purse, and shoes. Of course, she was wearing her own Genusee-made, vintage-style round frames. She's a role model in this midsized city, one of the nation's poorest, which is finding a new path forward. I had purposely come to one of the hardest-hit places in the Rust Belt because that's where the most extraordinary stories of turnaround happen. Ali Rose represents a fresh generation of talent returning home to help revive the industrial Midwest rather than running to the bright lights and big city. She would be one of many trailblazers I discovered on my grassroots journey through the heartland.

Having no business experience before didn't stop her. She enrolled in a retail tech accelerator in New York and was awarded $20,000 and a twenty-three-week mentorship when she won a design contest. A quick learner, she launched a Kickstarter crowdfunding campaign that surpassed her wildest expectations, exceeding a $50,000 goal and pulling in $74,000 in preorder sales within thirty days. Less than a month later, she made the brave move to Flint, far from the flash of Manhattan, to run her own business in a Rust Belt city reeling from job losses and a public-health crisis over tainted drinking water. Within a few months, her website, production, and online orders were up and running. It was the most challenging and rewarding experience of her life.

Genusee is proving that it's possible to scale up a small but meaningful business far from the garages and college dorms of Silicon Valley, Boston, and New York City—and in the neediest places. "The most rewarding part of the journey is shifting my values about work and the quality of life," Ali Rose told me. A former clothing designer, she had been profiled in *Vogue* as a top fashion disrupter, a tribute to the spread of creativity outside the usual runways of Los Angeles and New York. "I'm not so motivated by money. Building something for nothing motivates me," she said, adding, "It's an entrepreneurial disease."

Her eyeglass design is branded Roeper, named after the progressive school she attended in suburban Detroit, founded in 1941 by a Jewish couple who fled Nazi Germany. "We, rather than I," is how she described the learning environment at the school, a philosophy that she carries over into her business. She tries to do well by doing good. "In the 1970s, over half of Flint's population worked in manufacturing jobs, and today only about 12 percent do. Many of these people have been displaced and can't find jobs that fit their skill sets. People here know how to work with their hands and make things," she explained. "Most of our supply chain is within a thirty-mile radius and all our assembly line work is here."

Genusee is addressing the world's huge recycling challenge by using the leftovers of the Flint water crisis. Its production process includes purchasing empty water bottles from two Flint collectors. The plastics are catalyzed into pellets that are injection-molded into the circular shape and then sanded, buffed, and assembled with Italian-imported hinges. Prescription lenses are made by a separate lab. Each frame recycles fifteen single-use plastic water bottles. Genusee also buys back used frames and gives customers a credit toward a new pair. The used frames are also recycled. At the height of the crisis, Flint residents used twenty million water bottles daily, and it takes 450 years for one of those bottles to decompose in a landfill. Only 25 percent are recycled nationally.

Ali Rose's mission attracted seed funding from the social impact investor ImpactAssets and Michigan Rise and Invest Detroit Ventures, state-supported funds. More money poured in from angel investors, including Robert Wolf, a former UBS chief executive and Obama economic adviser, who had formed a Flint accelerator group, 100K Ventures, in partnership with a local philanthropist, Phil Hagerman. Wolf's interest had been piqued when he participated in a Comeback Capital tour of five Rust Belt cities, including Flint, in late 2018. In turn, several commercial and political leaders and professional athletes signed on as 100K Ventures founding members, including Super Bowl champion Victor Cruz, former Philadelphia mayor Michael Nutter, and Reshma Saujani, founder of the nonprofit organization Girls Who Code.

Her fund-raising from more influential angel investors continued through the COVID pandemic. "Raising money during the pandemic has been a journey," she said. But she believed in her success and predicted that, with steady growth, her business model could be replicated elsewhere.

Apart from raising money, Ali Rose has to run the business. She is hands-on, shipping products to retail boutiques and keeping up with individual orders with her crew of five local workers. Despite these pressures, she keeps innovating. She's expanded the product line to recycled cotton bags and totes and created bold new frames, including a Halloween-inspired black model with dark orange lenses. Genusee sunglasses were recently featured in a gift guide by Katie Couric as a must-have item for style and social impact.

Fulfilling her pledge to give back to the community, Ali Rose is donating 1 percent of profits to a Flint fund to improve children's education and health, providing for victims suffering from the long-lasting consequences of drinking polluted water. "It's hard work and the transition to Flint was tough," she acknowledged. "But I've never been happier, doing something that I thought was a dream. My goal has been to do good for people and the planet."

Flint's entrepreneurial reawakening owes much to Phil Hagerman. Ali Rose might not have gotten ahead in this down-and-out city without the master plan of his innovation catalyst, Skypoint Ventures, which has transformed the city's downtown blocks into an entrepreneurial zone. Hagerman invested $15 million to restore two historic abandoned buildings into a coworking space and startup boutique. A former retail store that had been vacant for thirty years became the Ferris Wheel innovation hub, where Genusee and another startup, which builds charging hubs for electric ride-sharing scooters, have set up shop. Next door a five-story, 1902 structure that had been a General Motors office and later a JCPenney department store was transformed into a pop-up shop for local business owners to sell their wares. Upstairs is Hagerman's office, where he nurtures new business concepts and funds the best ideas. He also donated two million dollars to establish the Hagerman Center for Entrepreneurship and Innovation at the University of Michigan's Flint campus. He is helping to rebuild the place where he grew up—a great example of how the Rust Belt is coming back.

Ali Rose was typical of what was to come: My meeting with dozens of talented, determined, out-of-the-box creators who have powered up small businesses in the toughest places, from industrial ghost towns to off-the-grid Appalachian Mountain communities. Entrepreneurship here doesn't fit the Silicon Valley's get-rich-quick mold. Experience and capital can still be lacking in the Midwest, but it's gaining in force.

Dayton: Taking Off

From Flint I headed south to Dayton to continue my survey of the diverse faces of Middle America's changing dynamic. The place was high on my itinerary. This southwestern Ohio city is where my journalistic career began as a Dow Jones editorial fellow before my senior college year, working the evening shift on the copy edit desk at the *Dayton Journal Herald,* racing against deadlines. As the glory days of newspaper publishing began to fade in the mideighties, the *Journal* was merged with the *Dayton Daily News* to become a morning-only edition. By then I'd left for Manhattan. In 2020, former owner Cox Enterprises repurchased the *Daily News* from a private equity investor—good news for Dayton, which had risked losing local newspaper coverage.

And there has been a lot to cover. In the early twentieth century, Dayton boasted the most patents per capita in the nation. Today it is striving to again become a leading innovation capital, to regain that illustrious past. Local residents Orville and Wilbur Wright invented the airplane, Charles Kettering developed the electric ignition starter for the automobile, and NCR made the first cash registers powered by an electric motor. To get a sense of that past, I visited the Wright Brothers Cycle Company, dating back to the 1890s, where the brothers capitalized on the cycling boom by making a safer-to-ride bike, ran a printing shop, and began experimenting with building gliders.

The two-story brick structure, though listed as a National Historic Landmark and once full of artifacts of the Wrights' aviation studies, had been approved by the city for demolition. I also saw evidence of a more recent downturn when I walked around the sprawling, park-like former headquarters of NCR, which moved to Atlanta in 2009 after 118 years, lured away with an incentive package and better civic amenities. Some 1,200 workers lost their jobs or were uprooted in that relocation, which shocked the city. NCR was the last of six Fortune 500 companies that left Dayton during the Rust Belt years.

But that was the past. What I really wanted to explore was the future. Today, the Miami Valley region in southwestern Ohio is moving forward with high-tech startups, an emerging innovation district, urban redevelopment, and an inventive culture. A major feeder is the Wright-Patterson Air Force Base, the region's biggest employer with 32,000 workers. Within its gates is the colossal Air Force Research Laboratory, which controls $2 billion for science and technology as well as funding small businesses, and the nineteen-acre National Museum of the US Air Force, featuring exhibits of 360 aerospace vehicles and military missiles.

My first entrepreneurial meeting in Dayton was with Nicholas Ripplinger, who had been wounded while serving with the US Army in Iraq. He'd returned to his hometown to start his own business and in 2017 launched Battle Sight Technologies, a manufacturer of night vision security devices. Ripplinger had accessed licensing technology from the air force and leveraged state government grants to get his business off the ground, and by the time I met him he had secured multiple military contracts for his business. "In the military, I was taught never to quit and never to fail," he told me. "I've applied these same concepts to my startup." He's not alone. Veteran-owned businesses make up nearly 6 percent of all US businesses.[15]

Ripplinger's mentor, Scott Koorndyk, is executive director of the Entrepreneurs' Center, the metro's leading technology business incubator. Opened in 2010, the center has fortified dozens of startups. One of its specialties is transferring technology and R&D from the Air Force Research Laboratory and working with entrepreneurs to spin out products commercially. Battle Sight Technologies started at the center's shared work space, strategically located midway between downtown and the base, in a former warehouse and light manufacturing district that's being transformed into a mixed-use urban neighborhood of startups, residences, and shops. As an entrepreneur in residence, Ripplinger got access to state-supported training, legal services, and seed capital. He sealed his first licensing deal with the Air Force Research Lab in 2017 and has piled on more.

Koorndyk has been tracking the progress of his protégé. "He got bit by the entrepreneurial bug," he said. "Dayton was hit so hard by the decline of manufacturing. The entrepreneurial culture was low, but now we are reenergizing it."

Meeting at the center, the former squad leader demonstrated his company's main device, the crayon-shaped CrayTac. In a dark, curtained booth in his lab, I put on night vision goggles to detect infrared marks visible only in the dark or in low light. Designed for the military, law enforcement agencies, and first responders, CrayTac is a lightweight, low-cost device that allows users to secure locations and mark routes and hazards. Another of his signaling markers is Nightfall, which can be used to rescue downed pilots at sea.

Ripplinger's friendly face belied his toughness. He served seven years in the army, including twenty-six months of combat duty in Iraq that ended when his leg was shattered. After a surgical rod was inserted to repair the damage, he spent several years in Germany in charge of protective services for the European command, before medically retiring in 2011. He moved back to Dayton with his wife to start a family, landed a couple of contracting jobs, and earned a degree in technical management.

But the former soldier was feeling "burned out and tapped out." Searching for something more professionally fulfilling, he wrote a book, *Front Line Strategies*, offering snapshots from ground fighting and lessons about applying military skills to entrepreneurship, like making calculated risk decisions. Though that earned him recognition, it hardly paid the bills. While promoting his book, he met Bennett Tanton, a former reconnaissance marine who hosted a podcast popular with veterans. Tanton became his business partner.

The two founders bootstrapped their startup and, since they haven't raised venture capital, own it outright. This would be highly unusual in Silicon Valley circles but not in the lower-cost Midwest, where government support has been an aid. In its first year, Battle Sight was awarded a $100,000 grant from the state-backed Ohio Third Frontier Commission to test the technology and develop a prototype for CrayTac. The business received a second grant for another signaling product. Dipping into the nearby resources, the startup secured an air force contract through an inaugural pitch day and contest open to American small businesses with the goal of furthering national security in air, space, and cyberspace. Competing against more than 400 contenders, the security device maker won $65,000 on the spot and ninety days later a further $100,000.

The company signed an international sales and distribution agreement with tech defense specialist Steiner eOptics, owned by firearms manufacturer Beretta Group. But as the coronavirus raged in 2020, the company's sales goal was missed. Ripplinger's survival skills kicked in. He shifted some production to hand sanitizers for emergency first responders and obtained a $56,000 loan under the federal government's paycheck protection program to keep his small team employed.

Rebounding in 2021, Battle Sight was one of eight participants in an inaugural nine-week federal government–funded defense accelerator program, designed to help startups get their technologies to market. Ripplinger has since outgrown his crowded space at the center and moved to a redeveloped building, the Manhattan, named after its historic research role in the Manhattan Project. Vacant for decades, the rundown structure was rehabbed specifically for tech startups.

I left Dayton with a good feeling about Battle Sight's prospects—and the city's. Linked to military and government support as the backbone of its operation, the company is geared to reach the next level, creating more jobs, revenues, and regional economic growth. The product lineup is being expanded to additional signaling tools. As we said good-bye, Ripplinger left me with positive words: "Doing a startup still feels like being in the fight, but it's not with guns and grenades. It's with technology."

Indianapolis: Nifty Training Software

Driving west on Interstate 70 from Dayton, I passed cornfield after cornfield. It was hypnotic. But major intersections and skyscrapers in the distance let me know that a big city was coming up. A lot of people were sheltering at home, so traffic was light and I reached downtown quickly and easily. Indianapolis. I wasn't in the cornfields now but in a fast-growing capital city of nearly 890,000.[16]

On my first evening there I walked around. I found Indy, as it's known, to be a surprisingly progressive and vibrant city. Bars along the popular Mass Avenue cultural district were filled with millennial couples and groups of gay men. Not many tourists around, but then the city's most famous attraction, the Indianapolis Motor Speedway, where the Indy 500 is held, was closed due to the epidemic. Later in my stay, I would get a chance to stand on the top row of the stadium and peer at the famous circuit.

But first I had my own circuit to complete. The following morning, the hotel receptionist handed out breakfast snacks in a paper bag, since all the property's restaurants were closed and few other guests were around. I ate quickly in the lobby, then headed across town to meet tech entrepreneur Max Yoder. I arrived at his work space in an old schoolhouse northeast of downtown in a neighborhood primed for revitalization. He rode his bicycle over to meet me at the front door, where a guard let us into the space.

Taking me on a tour of the converted school building, Yoder paused to play a classical tune on a grand piano he'd inherited when he moved in. As we walked around, I took in telltale signs of a fast-growth company, reminiscent of Silicon Valley. Wasn't this Indianapolis? There were the requisite ping-pong table, Peloton exercise bikes, and an open kitchen with free coffee and snacks. Posters and Post-it notes on display emphasized altruistic values: *highlight what's working, share before you are ready, have difficult conversations, make time for life.*

Everyone was working from home to stop the spread of the virus, so we sat in an empty room to talk about what prompted Yoder to start his own business. Going to work for his dad, who owned a funeral home, "never appealed to me," he said, deadpan. His first startup failed and took all his savings. But he stayed persistent. For his second try, he leaned on a tight-knit group of experienced local cofounders as mentors and investors who had cashed in when giant tech company Salesforce bought their email marketing service, ExactTarget, for $2.5 billion—an unprecedented amount for a Midwest tech company. And as Syam Nair, executive vice president of Salesforce, put it, "The acquisition of ExactTarget was definitely a catalyst and created a lot of interest in Indianapolis as an attractive tech hub."

Yoder leveraged that creative environment to launch Lessonly, an online software service for employee sales training at small and medium-sized businesses. He positioned it to fill a gap in the $31 billion elearning segment of the fast-expanding, $157 billion software-as-a-service market (SaaS). (I thought Salesforce might swoop in to buy Lessonly. My instincts about this up-and-coming company proved right, though I got the buyer wrong.)

A Hoosier from the small northern town of Goshen, Yoder earned a liberal arts degree at Indiana University in Bloomington, studying business, advertising, communications, and sociology. His thirst for entrepreneurship was whetted when he landed a two-year Orr Fellowship, named after former Indiana governor Robert Orr and designed to develop and recruit Indiana's next generation of business leaders and entrepreneurs. This gave Yoder a chance to work with Chris Baggott, an influential tech entrepreneur, founder of Compendium Software, and one of the cofounders of ExactTarget.

Yoder worked hard to pay off his student loans, saved his pennies, and poured his life savings into his first business, Quipol, a social polling tool for online publishers. But after an eighteen-month ride, he shut it because "publishers didn't have the appetite to pay." Lessonly also had roots in the Orr Fellowship. His cofounders were all fellow classmates in the two-year program.

It took nine months for Lessonly to gain traction, but within a decade it had ballooned to a 240-employee business with four million individual customers and 1,200 enterprise clients, including Dun & Bradstreet, Goodwill, and US Cellular. Using a subscription model, the company marketed six-step lesson plans with real-life practice sessions, role-playing, feedback loops, and quizzes for retention. Yoder's multidisciplinary college studies paid off in well-conceived brand messaging and design elements. The company motto was *Do better work and live better lives*. The software design was bright and friendly.

In 2015, TechPoint, Indiana's growth accelerator for startups, awarded Lessonly startup of the year. Yoder went on to raise $30 million in venture capital, most of it initially from that inner circle of cofounders and colleagues at ExactTarget. Such an approach to deal-making may sound clubby, but it was a good indication of the success of the Midwest's growing tech environment. In California it happens a lot, as when the so-called PayPal mafia of cofounders cashed out and proceeded to launch such impactful startups as Tesla, LinkedIn, Palantir, and SpaceX.

Over the next two years, Lessonly flew the nest and pulled in funding from two outside venture capital firms, OpenView in Boston and Rethink Education in New York. Just before sheltering in place began in April 2020, Yoder snagged a just-in-time $15 million investment that wrapped in two significant Bay Area players: AXA Venture Partners and customer relations service Zendesk as a strategic investor. The team maneuvered through the challenging COVID outbreak by shifting to online training for remote work. In July 2021, Lessonly acquired Canadian software maker Obie to round out product offerings for hybrid work, and a month later Lessonly itself was acquired by the San Diego–based sales marketing platform Seismic, a former major customer with an aligned business mission. The deal put Lessonly in a growing league of young businesses in the Midwest that excelled at maximizing their value.

Calling it a "dream outcome," Yoder predicted the acquisition was bound to have a ripple effect in the region. He and his core founding team are staying in Indianapolis. As I was closing my laptop and getting ready to leave for my next interview in town, he handed me a copy of his book about finding clarity, camaraderie, and progress, *Do Better Work*. I've kept it on my bookshelf, a symbol of can-do spirit and the importance of community support in the emerging tech market of the Midwest.

Pittsburgh: From Steel to R&D

After Indianapolis, I returned to Lancaster to plot my next stop in Pittsburgh. Rather than compete with speeding cargo trucks on I-70, I decided to follow the less-traveled country route, a detour that might have taken me longer but allowed for all sorts of new sights. On the way, I wanted to check out a shale gas operation that is unleashing a new source of energy, replacing coal-fired plants.

In southeastern Ohio's Appalachian Basin, I met Eddy Biehl, a geologist who owns the oil and natural gas business Stonebridge Operating, which goes back several generations to the 1870s and has nearly a thousand wells in six counties. He showed me around the truck yard, filled with lots of big, mysterious-looking trucking, piping, and drilling equipment behind a chain-link fence. He readily explained the boom and bust cycles of pricing over his forty years in the business. Thrilled to learn about this fracking business in a remote area, I was reminded of covering China's scrappy tech entrepreneurship in the early days, before it became more corporate.

Eddy's business was a good reminder of where this country had been and where it was going. Over hills on winding roads, I reached the Ohio River Valley in Marietta at the mouth of the Muskingum River, bordering West Virginia. Following the river northward on Route 7, I passed coal-fired power plants and chemical factories from the industrial development of small towns and rural communities in a postwar economic boom. It was a perfect day, blue sky and puffy white clouds. The contrast was stark at ground level. I stopped to take photos of thick smoke spewing from coal-plant smokestacks. I could smell sulfur in the air.

Then on to Pittsburgh on Route 70 and Highway 79, past corporate parks, suburban houses, and franchise hotels. Through the Fort Pitt tunnel and out the other side on the Fort Pitt Bridge, and there suddenly was the skyline of Pittsburgh, with the distinctive PPG Industries skyscraper at its center, the air now clear where there used to be smoke-blackened skies. Continuing on past several river bends,

I stopped at the industrial borough of Braddock, ten miles out of Pittsburgh along the Monongahela River. Here is US Steel's hulking, ghostly Edgar Thomson Works. Once one of many day-and-night operations along the Monongahela, it's the last of the city's steel mills still firing. Next to it is a New Age startup: Fifth Season, run by AI-powered robots and cultivated from the tech-rich environment of Carnegie Mellon University.

Pittsburgh once produced half the nation's steel. Its mills made the girders to support the Empire State Building and the Golden Gate Bridge, and it employed close to 300,000. But when four main steel plants were closed in the early eighties, unemployment in the area topped 18 percent. Between 1970 and 1990, the region lost 158,000 manufacturing jobs, and 289,000 metropolitan residents left for brighter locales[17] while 30 percent of the city's population moved out.

On the drive to Braddock, I saw the fallout: boarded-up homes, littered streets, broken sidewalks, and poor folks hanging out aimlessly on weather-beaten front porches. It was hard to imagine that this once-thriving, now-decimated community is where Andrew Carnegie operated his first steel mill along the banks of the river in the 1870s.

Now, rebuilders of business and residential developments and twenty-first-century tech entrepreneurs are bringing back the borough. Fifth Season is an automated vegetable-growing vertical farm in an indoor, half-acre facility powered by artificial intelligence and robots (and only a few dozen employees). I had come here to meet its founder, Austin Webb.

"We are going from seed to harvest to packaging," Webb said as he led me past the high-ceilinged growing room equipped with solar panels, long conveyor belts, and LED light bulbs. "The vegetables that we produce are a new definition of freshness, and we do it with less water, less land, and efficiently and safely. We are bringing in New Age agriculture jobs to the city that never existed before and bridging to the workforce of the future. Our smart manufacturing facility improves the yield, taste, and texture of the vegetables, and does that with 95 percent less water and 99 percent less land, and uses no pesticides or chemicals."

It took two years of research and development on the south side of Pittsburgh in a converted steel mill before tests proved that the robotics vertical farm could work on a larger scale. Webb relocated his upstart to greenfield space in this Braddock warehouse in summer 2020. "I wanted to go into a community down on its luck and help solve problems," said Webb. He pointed out that Braddock doesn't have a grocery store if you don't count Family Dollar. "There are very resilient people here."

Webb is a transplant to Pittsburgh from Chapel Hill, North Carolina. He was drawn to social impact, technology, and entrepreneurship. A finance major at Wofford College in Spartanburg, South Carolina, Webb started his career as a financial analyst at Lockheed Martin, then spent five years as an investment banker in Washington, DC. Several of his clients ran small-to-medium-sized businesses, and Webb began thinking, Why couldn't he? He earned an MBA at Carnegie Mellon's Tepper School of Business. Now, his high-tech startup seems destined to help solve global food problems. And it's in a hot market sector that's forecast to double in size to $16 billion by 2025.[18]

But it's not without risks. Fifth Season is in a capital-intensive business that needs real estate, a building, and a team of engineers to keep operations running smoothly at a high-quality level. It's a highly competitive, expanding business sector, and a land grab for regional leadership is going on. That's why this newcomer stayed in stealth mode until its technology was validated.

Pittsburgh is the leading national hub for AI and robotics. So Fifth Season uses forty-five "bots" and QR bar codes on every tray to track thousands of data points such as air temperature, humidity, and light spectrum. The fully robotic operation is housed in a 60,000-square-foot, solar-powered warehouse. "We track every moment of the plant's life," Webb told me. "Working alongside their robot friends, only about twenty-five human workers are needed to check on equipment, cleaning, and maintenance." Some 500,000 pounds of leafy greens were grown in the first year, and there's potential for expansion to nearby cities. "We have the blueprints and can scale up, through rinse and repeat," he said.

High costs have been a major limitation to wide acceptance of hydroponically grown produce compared with farm-grown field greens. By relying on proprietary technologies that monitor the plants, Fifth Season can cultivate produce at prices that are competitive with "Farmer Brown" conventional crops. "Growing up, my brother and I never dreamed we would become modern-day farmers," said Webb, whose father is a teacher and his mother a lawyer. He acknowledged that he's more of a meat eater than a vegetable lover, but now, surrounded by all those fresh greens, he eats salads several times a week. Fifth Season sells its flavorful spinach, arugula, and herbs to Whole Foods, Giant Eagle, and other grocery stores, local restaurants, and on-campus dining locations. It's also launched an e-commerce business with Pittsburgh-area deliveries.

The Carnegie Mellon network proved to be a lifeline for Webb. While still a student, he developed a prototype, found mentors, and got work space at CMU's Swartz Center for Entrepreneurship. This multidisciplinary business, technology, and startup center, established in 2015 through a $31 million gift by venture capitalist James R. Swartz of Accel, boosted the university's ranking nationally in entrepreneurship. Webb also relied on campus connections to raise an initial million dollars from Robotics Hub, an accelerator and venture firm founded by CMU business school graduates and GE Ventures. The capital landed on day two of his second year in the MBA program.

Through the entrepreneurship center's executive director, Dave Mawhinney, Webb linked up with Drive Capital, a Columbus-based firm and a key investor in the region's most promising tech startups. Drive Capital led a $35 million co-investment in Fifth Season; other funding of $40 million came from Pritzker-connected Tao Capital, angel investors with close ties to the university; and debt financing came from Silicon Valley Bank.

This robust network effect of collaboration continued to work, just as it does in Stanford circles in Silicon Valley. Mawhinney introduced Webb to the serial entrepreneur Luis von Ahn, who created the spam protectors Captcha and reCaptcha, as well as the online language learning app Duolingo. Von Ahn became a mentor to Webb and an angel investor. "I always tell entrepreneurs that we still live in a world where the most important thing for a startup is who you know, because a lot of decisions are based on trust and respect," Mawhinney said. He continued to offer his support, later investing in Fifth Season and becoming a board adviser.

Webb took a giant risk building Fifth Season in the transitioning Braddock community. But now his venture is inspiring other startups to set up in Rust Belt Pennsylvania, drawn by the low costs and a scrappy, atmospheric vibe portrayed in the 2013 movie *Out of the Furnace*. About a mile down the road, I met another brave soul, tech founder Jim Gibbs. Originally from Long Island, he attended Carnegie Mellon and stayed. He's the charismatic coder and a force behind startup MeterFeeder, an EZ Pass–type app for parking.

Build Back Better

Down-and-out places such as Braddock and Flint are recovering with more than hopes and dreams, thanks to hardworking, resilient people who are opportunistically taking a chance on starting up in rough terrain. As startups in these towns progress well outside Silicon Valley's domain, and more abandoned sites are reused, a new era built upon innovative ideas born from an economic wasteland is emerging.

This tough transition is part of a renewal that is allowing Middle America to build back better after too many years of hardship. As I left Pittsburgh and continued my heartland odyssey into postindustrial Ohio, I celebrated this long-awaited change to the state where I grew up. My travels would lead me to Youngstown and Ironton, two hardened industrial towns grappling with change and seeking to forge ahead with game-changers in nearly forgotten hinterlands. Their old factories couldn't be more of a contrast with Apple's satellite-shaped headquarters in Cupertino, where the next I-gadget was no doubt being invented. But they were making a game of it.

Chapter Two

Allies in Industrial Innovation

*How industrialist innovators are partnering with corporate America
to revive the Rust Belt with startups, from plastic recyclers to
manufacturers of electric pickup trucks*

My circuit through the heartland brought me face-to-face with some of
the region's most innovative entrepreneurs. They gave me a great sense
of the energy—the *reenergy*—that is fueling the Midwest's comeback.
That positive vibe was reaffirmed as well by long-standing companies
that were reenergizing the Rust Belt with a new model of innovation,
one that matches startup innovators with corporate powerhouses such
as Procter & Gamble (P&G), General Motors, Eli Lilly, and others.

I met this model from the start. From my home base in Lancaster, I had
driven for two hours to the southernmost point of Ohio, the rural Hanging
Rock region in the foothills of Appalachia. Along the way, I passed Chilli-
cothe, the home of a paper-making mill that we used to call "Stinktown"
for the foul stench that blasted out of the iconic red-and-white smokestacks. Holding my nose, I sped by on the Route 23 bypass and continued
south, the rolling hills of the Appalachian Plateau ahead of me.

A Game-changing Technology

My first destination was off the beaten track, in an industrial zone
close to Ironton. Not many people knew of PureCycle Technologies,

but it was about to take off with an inventive process for recycling rigid plastics that pollute our oceans and lands. My research had put the company on my radar, and I was eager to investigate it firsthand.

A regional business consultant had tried to discourage me. "You don't want to go there!" she said. "It's dirty." That made me all the more curious. Through a series of blind calls to the plant, I got connected to human resources and then the facility manager, who relayed me to the offsite CEO, Mike Otworth, an experienced industrial innovator. We spoke by phone and made arrangements to meet.

PureCycle Technologies sits on a sixty-five-acre industrial tract bordering a huge power plant in Haverhill, Ohio. Dow Chemical had employed two hundred workers here making Styrofoam plastics until a restructuring and shutdown in 2016. PureCycle had stepped in with a business plan calling for at least fifty full-time workers making $40,000 a year, a good wage in the region.

I pulled into the complex and parked near a small-scale, aluminum-sided building labeled *feedstock evaluation unit.* This windowless facility didn't look dirty from the outside, but what was going on inside was positively filthy. "Feedstock" refers not to your everyday household garbage but stuff like tossed-out carpets and old auto interiors that are being fed in for recycling.

In an adjacent building's conference room, Otworth filled me in. This groundbreaking operation had an exclusive global license to commercialize a patented P&G technology that addresses a far-from-solved problem. Most rigid plastics are recycled through a mechanical grinding process that results in a dark, smelly, low-value product. PureCycle's process instead produces purified, packaging-ready recycled resin that is like-new quality with no colors, odors, or contaminants. The business potential is huge; long-lasting, rigid polypropylene is the most common type of plastic worldwide, but less than 1 percent of it gets recycled. By contrast, about 30 percent of other, more common plastics used for bottles and consumer goods is reused. PureCycle Technologies is aiming to eventually recycle 10 to 20 percent of the tougher plastics.

"PureCycle Technologies is solving the big problem of these wastes getting into landfills, leaking into the environment, getting into our waterways, and creating pollution," Otworth told me. He showed me the tiny, clear pellets that remain after the purifying magic does its trick. "There is too much plastic waste and low-quality plastic waste. This new recycling innovation will help fix our broken trash system. This is a new approach. This is the type of innovation you need to solve a major problem in a new way."

I called Steve Alexander, president and CEO of the Association of Plastic Recyclers in Washington, DC, for validation. "This is a big deal," he told me. "It's a technology game-changer. They have the innovation and now they need to scale up. I don't know of any other company with technology that can do this kind of recycling." Indeed, *Time* magazine named PureCycle's patented technology one of 2019's top one hundred inventions.

PureCycle is based in the Hanging Rock region, which takes its name from a large sandstone cliff. It is also known as the iron-producing capital of the United States. When technology converted to steel-making and abundant iron ore was depleted, dozens of charcoal-fired blast furnaces stopped firing in southern Ohio, and the industry died out by 1916. All that is left today of the iron-makers is tall, crumbling stone stacks covered with weeds. The once-dynamic Ironton (a contraction of *iron* and *town*) wasn't able to pivot to the new, higher-potential industry. Like many other Rust Belt places, it stayed stuck in the past. As I drove through the region, I remembered my parents pointing out Buckeye Furnace and the remains of the state's nineteenth-century iron industry when we went down home to my grandparents' farm.

As manufacturing and mining jobs disappeared over the past several decades, Ironton's population declined by one-third to 11,000. More than a quarter of its residents live in poverty.[19] It's no different in the surrounding Lawrence and Scioto Counties: a declining population suffering from poverty, chronic unemployment, low education levels, poor nutrition, and drug addiction.[20]

The once-booming county seat of Ironton still has its storied brick homes of the iron barons, the domed roof of the Greek Revival courthouse, and several huge Bible Belt churches—but these are symbols of a faded past. The new Ironton is a contemporary retail sprawl of Walmart, McDonald's, and discount outlets like Dollar General and Family Dollar. It was depressing and shocking to see so many vacated farm homes, weathered barns about to collapse, rusted-out cars, and help signs for recovering drug addicts. But I also spotted signs of regeneration: spruced-up downtowns, renovations of historic buildings and railroad stations, and career training centers.

Partnering Makes Good

PureCycle's licensing of a P&G technology is a good example of how many Rust Belt tech-smart upstarts are innovating by partnering with large, resource-rich, well-capitalized corporations. Young businesses are gaining market access, customers, facilities, and industry expertise—and the reputational boost of partnering with major corporate players. These innovators promise to get the region humming again.

Labor forces in capital-intensive, R&D-rich business sectors are powering a reboot of the Rust Belt. It's nothing like the crypto-crazy, metaverse mind-set of Silicon Valley. The pace is slower and the process can be more complex and certainly more down-to-earth. Compared with the Sand Hill Road epicenter, venture capital in the "mighty middle" states is still sparse. But investment in the region has increased by a factor of four, and thousands of deals have been made over the past decade. Momentum is building. Unicorn-valued startups, high-ticket acquisitions, and IPOs have popped up in

---

Tech Tools in the Rust Belt

Tech innovators in the industrialized beltway of the Midwest are using an array of tools to turn the region's prospects around:

- repurposing abandoned plants and sites
- leveraging large corporate resources
- raising millions from IPOs, loans, and bonds
- investing heavily in R&D
- integrating digital technologies
- licensing patented technology
- rehiring laid-off workers
- retraining fresh graduates in technical skills
- launching new businesses in places with limited job opportunities

Pittsburgh, Columbus, Indianapolis, and Detroit. A Tech Belt quite distinct from Silicon Valley is replacing the Rust Belt.

Flyover country, as it's been ridiculed by the Silicon Valley elite, has a long road to recovery. There are too many minimum-wage positions, which don't come close to replacing the thousands of lost higher-paying manufacturing jobs. Many inner cities and rural towns in the heartland struggle with talented folks leaving, weak or no broadband, and a diminishing tax base. But with the entrepreneurial spirit alive and well in metros like Youngstown, and politicians like Tim Ryan fighting to transform his old-line manufacturing district into a mighty Tech Belt, there may be a shot at creating a brighter future.

PureCycle grew out of Innventure, a joint venture that Mike Otworth set up with Greg Wasson, the retired CEO of Walgreens, and his family investment office, Wasson Enterprise. In a fresh approach, Innventure identifies promising enterprise technologies and patents at large companies and forms tech startups to develop their intellectual property, and—if all goes well—launches billion-dollar businesses with risk lower than you usually have with a traditional venture-capital model.

Otworth grew up near Columbus, not far from my own hometown. After graduation he began his career working as a legislative aide on Capitol Hill, but he gravitated to social-impact investment businesses. He selected southern Ohio as a base for PureCycle because he wanted to give back to the place where he'd spent a good part of his childhood, visiting his grandparents in nearby Portsmouth well before the factories closed and the city bottomed out. We connected because of our shared roots. "I remember when the economics here were much better, and I'd really love to see it return to the way it used to be. That was part of our motivation for wanting to locate here," Otworth told me. "This is my 'give back' strategy."

A pragmatic executive who gets things done, his skills fit the large task of contributing to recovery in this industrial wasteland. His track record includes evaluating and vetting disruptive technologies with Fortune 50 companies, including Eli Lilly. He's also scaled up or taken public eleven emerging tech startups in the fields of biology, healthcare, and the environment.

"We work with a handful of multinationals with a lot of break-throughs in research and development to do things like this with P&G and others," he said. "It's not something we can do on our own." His eyes lit up when I mentioned that I was planning to meet Valarie Sheppard, who was overseeing P&G's financial commitment to innovations.[21] P&G is at the forefront of out-of-the-box transformative approaches to ventures.

As the manufacturer of best-selling brands such as Tide, Downy, Ivory, and Pampers, P&G has a big incentive to support recycling, and the company has a goal of 100 percent recyclable or renewable plastics by 2030. "We look to partner with investors and startups not just for a financial return but for access to innovation. I have to make the case: is the technology translating into something we can integrate into P&G?" Sheppard and I spoke at the company's head-quarters in Cincinnati. From the progress I had seen at PureCycle Technologies, it looked like she knew how to make the right call. P&G is also working with Innventure and an Orlando-based business, AeroFlexx, to introduce flexible packaging for bottling Old Spice cologne and Dawn liquid dish soap. In another collaboration with PureCycle, P&G's sustainable personal-care line EC30 launched a recycled plastic shower dispenser, made from souvenir cups collected at sports stadiums.

I also asked Bill Dingus, executive director of Lawrence County's Economic Development Corporation, about the impact of this partnership model in his region and beyond. He was highly enthusiastic. "It's phenomenal what [PureCycle and P&G] have done," he told me. "It's so timely for this country, and it will solve a problem for future generations. You have to wonder how many other technologies are lying around on shelves at corporations like P&G that we can bring to life."

Building out PureCycle was no easy feat. Construction costs for its first commercial-scale plant ran $363 million and entailed revitalizing three buildings on a twenty-three-acre industrial strip long targeted for redevelopment. Financing came from a $250 million bond offering and a $1.2 billion go-public deal via a special purpose acquisition company (SPAC). The stock trades on Nasdaq under the ticker symbol PCT.

State, regional, and local economic groups all kicked in initial funding. Lawrence County acquired the former Dow Chemical property. JobsOhio granted $750,000 for revitalization. An additional $3.5 million was slated for a sewer line extension, rails, and tapping into natural gas for onsite operations. A local business executive, Andy Glockner, owner of several auto dealerships in the tri-state area of Ohio, West Virginia, and Kentucky, wrote a $2 million check to decommission the old chemical plant on the site. Glockner's sons Tim and Joe sat in on my meeting at the site and proudly added that, as the sixth generation of Glockners in the region, they "felt an obligation to our own area." Otworth got connected with the Glockners at a meeting of the Port Authority of Southern Ohio. He appreciated their involvement. "My most important source of capital was right here in Portsmouth," he pointed out. "This business would not have been possible without their initial support."

PureCycle broke ground for a pilot facility in 2017 and planned to have its full-scale commercial plant recycling plastics by 2023. That was about two years behind the original timetable, as the engineering team mastered some technical challenges and worked to prove that the revolutionary process reliably worked. As Otworth put it, "If it were a science project, I wouldn't be involved."

"There's a lot of buzz and excitement about PureCycle," observed Greg Smithies, then a partner at corporate strategic investor BMW i Ventures. "It's taking garbage in, black, dirty, smelly plastic, and incredible crystal-clear pure resin is coming out the other side." Smithies believed that BMW might someday put PureCycle's recycled plastics into its vehicles.[22]

Now, it's all about executing on a monumental goal. Revenues of $800 million by 2024 are targeted, and profitability with 50 percent margins. By 2030, PureCycle aims to have thirty plants globally and an additional fifty within five years, including one in Japan, where it's recently formed a partnership with Mitsui & Co., and another under construction in Augusta, Georgia.

The company's first full-scale plant in Haverhill is slated to churn out more than 105 million pounds of ultrapure recycled polypropylene per year. That sounds like a lot but actually is a tiny portion of the annual 100 billion pounds of such waste accumulated globally. Beauty products maker L'Oreal already has agreed to buy nearly all of Pure-Cycle's initial supply. Potential demand far exceeds what this first facility can handle, Otworth noted optimistically. "Instead of mourning the loss of old industry, we are being proactive instead," he said. I was amazed how matter-of-fact he sounded when talking to me about such a game-changing challenge ahead.

Belt Buckle Stop

The following Sunday, I drove northeast from Ironton through central Ohio's Amish country, passing the clip-clop of horse-drawn buggies of traditional farming families going to church. I reached the point near where the Ohio & Erie Canal in the 1830s, and later the railroads and interstate highways, were plotted. The Mahoning River flows through this region, winding through a once-formidable economic zone of steel factories. Nearly half a million people live in this metro area, so when steel-mill closings left 40,000 out of work, it hit the region hard.[23]

But a new dawn was rising. Once known as Steel Valley, this flatland has now been rebranded Voltage Valley in honor of a new electrifying identity. Another moniker is the Belt Buckle, which marks its status as the hub of a sprawling region that once bustled with steel mills and auto factories and is now innovating. Proof of that innovative spark is GM's construction of a $2.3 billion joint venture plant to make electric battery cells. It will eventually employ 1,100 workers. And in nearby Warren, Brite Energy Innovators has incubated 400 energy tech startups in a former Kresge's department store, which have spawned at least 1,100 jobs.

Driving through the region on I-80, it's hard to miss the gigantic Lordstown Motors factory outside of Youngstown. About the size of a hundred football fields, it is situated on once-fertile farmland along Mahoning Valley's steel-making manufacturing corridor. Its entrance outside the village of Lordstown features a large billboard that used to proudly advertise GM's auto-producing plant as "Home of the Cruze." The sign, recently taken down, said "Ride with Lordstown."

I pulled into the nearly empty parking lot, here to interview Steve Burns, a nonconformist entrepreneur and business juggler. He created a glimmer of hope for the region by engineering the purchase of this massive factory, which left thousands of workers unemployed when it shut down. In its place, he launched Lordstown Motors as a maker of an electric-powered pickup truck, branded the Endurance.

Outfitted with goggles, helmet, mask, and an orange reflective vest, Burns took me on a golf-cart ride past the body and paint shops, metal stamping section, welding machines, and rows of caged robots. It was the first time I'd toured an auto assembly plant outside China. Blue-collar workers were nowhere to be seen. The last 1,500 of nearly 10,000 UAW members were let go in March 2019 when GM closed the plant after fifty-three years in this once-booming industrial zone.

"Can you believe we own all this? We are nimble like a startup but heavy in assets," Burns exclaimed, shouting over the loud, rhythmic hum of the 6.2-million-square-foot, 785-acre complex. "My dream is to fill this factory with workers," he added, grinning widely. He was gearing up to hire 1,500 employees by 2022—in synch with a Buy American agenda to boost the nation's industries. "We are getting there first and will have a first-mover advantage," he insisted.

A visionary wheeler-dealer and inventor who hardly fits the midwestern mold, Burns dabbled in futuristic, electric-powered vehicles such as the SureFly hybrid-electric, two-seater flying helicopter and the HorseFly delivery drone, which flies from the top of trucks. By far, the boldest move of his roller-coaster career was to swoop in and purchase GM's shuttered auto plant in late 2019, just a few months after it closed. It was an incredible bargain at $20 million, sweetened further with a $40 million GM loan.

Before the Lordstown project, Burns had started and sold three mobile software and digital advertising startups, one of them to media giant Gannett. He got into electric vehicles as CEO of AMP, an experimental developer of e-powered roadsters and delivery vans. In 2013, he acquired Workhorse Group, a Cincinnati-based maker of GM stepvan delivery trucks at a shut-down plant in Indiana. His objective was to produce electric-powered food trucks and delivery vans, but he was kicked out of the loss-making Workhorse operation in 2019, blamed for wasting money on side projects.

But Burns is an entrepreneur, and within months he had put together a complex transaction to buy the GM plant in northeast Ohio and start an offshoot of his prior business. Workhorse would get a 10 percent stake in his new entity, a $12.2 million licensing fee for its intellectual property, and a 1 percent commission on Endurance sales. His new business, Lordstown Motors, also was set to pick up 6,000 e-pickup preorders from Workhorse (which had lost a bid to build a next-generation mail truck for the USPS).

Needing cash to start production, Burns opted for a streamlined, popular process for becoming a publicly traded company called a SPAC and netted $675 million. GM contributed a token $75 million in the go-public transaction, and the startup began trading on Nasdaq under the ticker symbol RIDE.

Burns targeted the niche and steady market of commercial fleets rather than the more volatile consumer market. He priced the Endurance at a reasonable midrange of $52,500 and initially planned a production start date of September 2021. Bookings of 100,000 preorders showed demand for the EV truck, which can travel 250 miles on a full charge, get the equivalent of 75 miles of gas per gallon, and tow 7,500 pounds. The kicker is its four software-controlled electric motors within the pickup's wheel hubs, a technology previously used mainly for e-bikes.

Lordstown Motors hired five EV executives, including two engineering pros from Tesla. Allocations were made for production, inspection, testing, retooling, and R&D. Suppliers were lined up: Goodyear in nearby Akron for tires; Samsung for battery cells; Slovenia-based Elaphe for in-wheel hub motors; and GM for air bags, locks, and steering wheels.

Few vehicles had quite the publicity build-up as the Endurance. A few weeks before my own stop, then–vice president Mike Pence had visited Lordstown and ridden with Burns in a pickup prototype onto a makeshift stage decorated with an American flag. Pence spoke of how the reopened factory signified a revival of the region. "Endurance isn't just the name of the pickup truck; endurance describes the character of the people of the Mahoning Valley," Pence told the audience. "It's part of the great American comeback. The best days for Lordstown and Ohio and America are yet to come."

Burns followed this PR coup with an even bigger endorsement. In a preelection, campaign-like event not long afterward, then-president Donald Trump inspected the pickup parked on the South Lawn of the White House and raved about its features. "It's the first pickup truck with a trunk; it's in the front," Burns boasted. "So you can call it a 'frunk,' but you have to pronounce it carefully, right?" Trump agreed.

My golf-cart ride at Lordstown Motors was bumpy as Burns motored across a test-drive patch of gravel, dirt, and concrete, and my purse was almost tossed off the seat. As we said our good-byes at the factory entrance, Burns said, "My kids have gone from saying I'm crazy to saying I'm eccentric." I've heard that before from Silicon Valley denizens. Hearing it in the heartland seemed a hopeful sign of an entrepreneurial spirit on the rise.

The EV Future

The Rust Belt's decline and comeback has been a focus for the region's political leaders. Around this time I interviewed congressman Tim Ryan, who told me, "We need a national industrial policy to focus on domestic industries of the future and those communities that have been left behind, and the industrial losses of the past thirty to forty years." Ryan represented Ohio's thirteenth congressional district, where GM and related auto and steel industries once prospered. He has repeatedly campaigned on increased government investment to shift Ohio's traditional industries into new-economy jobs. "We need game-changing industries," he said. One of his areas of focus was the country's push for next-generation EV technologies and the urgency to out-compete China. "Why," Ryan asked me rhetorically, "should we let the electric vehicle market go to China?"

Good question! Community leaders and politicians are now promoting the rebranded Voltage Valley, with hopes that it can replace "about the same number of workers [as GM let go]," as then-senator from Ohio Rob Portman put it.[24] But success in such a competitive market isn't easy. Within months of my visit, and the Pence and Trump endorsements, Lordstown Motors was heading into a deep ditch. There were reports of fake orders and production hurdles, the Securities and Exchange Commission launched an investigation into misrepresentation of preorders, and the Justice Department started a criminal probe. The company warned that it needed more money to produce the Endurance and might not survive. Burns resigned and the board replaced him with CEO Daniel Ninivaggi, a former automotive executive within Carl Icahn's business empire.

In late 2021, the embattled truck maker got a second chance that could give Rust Belt Ohio a better shot at recovery. The Taiwanese technology firm Foxconn, a well-capitalized, tech-savvy maker of Apple's iPhone (which had retreated from plans to build a $10 billion LDC complex in Wisconsin), bought the Lordstown Motors plant for $230 million, with new plans to build the Endurance and a line of e-pickups on site under a joint venture. The whole episode has been a jolt for this depressed region, even if few expected a smooth ride.

In 2009, during the financial crisis, GM received $60.3 million in Ohio tax credits in exchange for keeping its Lordstown plant open for thirty years; but it closed the factory in 2019. With the Biden administration promising to revitalize the battered blue-collar region and create an estimated five million jobs in manufacturing and innovation throughout America, we haven't heard the end of this comeback story.

Lordstown Motors and other entrants into this important space have had their challenges. But there can be no doubt that we are heading into an automotive landscape dominated by electric vehicles. With lower fuel and maintenance costs, and the push for clean energy, these vehicles represent the future.[25] EVs are forecast to reach up to 30 percent of new car purchases nationally in 2030 and almost half by 2035.[26] And the United States is lagging behind, trailing Europe in the lead and China as second.[27] President Biden set an aggressive goal of having half of all new vehicles sold in 2030 be zero-emission, and he pledged more charging stations nationwide, tax incentives, and customer rebates, plus plug-in school buses and postal vans.

The Midwest is in a good position to capitalize on repurposed and reopened factories for a new transportation future. Alphabet's Waymo autonomous driving unit from Silicon Valley is reviving an idled Detroit factory to develop and make its self-driving electric vehicles. Kickstarting a new era, Ford's first battery-powered model of its popular F-150 Lightning pickup, produced in Michigan, went on sale in mid-2022 with a base price tag of $40,000. On a mission to go electric, GM has three e-pickups in the works at its upgraded, retrofitted Factory Zero plant in Detroit: its $100,000 Hummer EV pickup, which began deliveries in late 2021; a plug-in version of the GMC Sierra, planned for production in 2023; and the Chevrolet Silverado E in the first half of the year. Also in the race is Ford- and Amazon-backed e-truck maker Rivian, under contract to build 100,000 Amazon delivery vans at a previously shut plant near Chicago beginning in early 2023. Meanwhile, Tesla expects to debut its futuristic, techie-pleasing, all-electric Cybertruck in 2023 from its Gigafactory under construction in Austin.

Not all consumers like EVs. There's a huge cultural divide between rural regions and urban metros. Teslas are almost ordinary now in trend-conscious San Francisco, where EVs make up 11 percent of new vehicle sales. The smallest share for EVs is in the Midwest, at .8 percent.[28] My younger brother, who recently bought a hefty, gas-powered Toyota pickup, didn't even consider buying electric. He was aware of the pulling power and torque of electric trucks but thought the price tag was too high and that purchasing a brand-new vehicle with an untested technology was risky. Besides, there are too few charging stations near where he lives in Lancaster. The heartland is a great place to build EVs—now it has to become a great place to buy one.

A Cautionary Note

My trip through northern Ohio gave me many reasons to be optimistic—the entrepreneurial drive, the innovation, individuals and corporations looking for new ways to revitalize the region. But I was also aware of the scale of the challenge. After my Lordstown visit, I booked into a DoubleTree hotel in downtown Youngstown. The handsome 1908 building was once the headquarters for Youngstown Sheet & Tube, the Steel Valley's largest employer with 5,000 blue-collar workers. That mill closed in 1977, on a day that became known as Black Monday. Its failure was part of a rash of steel producers shutting in Youngstown and throughout the valley. The industrial stretch between Cleveland and Pittsburgh saw nearly 50,000 factory job losses in the 1970s as offshoring and imports rose.[29] Over forty-five years later, the region is still suffering from that blow.

From this low point, the Youngstown metro area is primed for revitalization to reverse declining population, lack of jobs, and poverty.[30] Looking out my hotel window, I could see Youngstown's solid hope for the future: a building housing an incubator group focused on made-in-America advanced manufacturing. But the road is long and bumpy, and revitalization is harder than many, including politicians, often realize. When Donald Trump campaigned in

About two-thirds of the 278 US auto plant dinosaurs have been repurposed and retrofitted in recent decades by EV makers.[31] Here are some examples.

- **Tesla** took over a closed GM-Toyota auto manufacturing plant in Fremont, California, in 2010 for a bargain $42 million. Today, the plant mass-produces its all-electric sedans with a large workforce of 10,000, nearly double the 4,500 who lost their jobs.
- **GM's** rebranded, all-electric Factory Zero in Detroit, which once made Chevrolets and Cadillacs as well as the Chevy Volt plug-in hybrid, has undergone a $2.2 billion retrofit to make its electric pickup trucks and SUVs, as well as a Cruise Origin driverless robotaxi. Some 2,200 employees are eventually expected when the plant is operating fully, roughly double the number prior to the factory retooling.
- **Rivian** paid $16 million to purchase a shut Chrysler-Mitsubishi plant in Normal, Illinois (southwest of Chicago), in 2017. Under a five-year tax abatement and a million-dollar grant, the EV upstart plans to invest $175 million in the factory and create 1,000 jobs by 2024 to make its vehicles.
- **GM's** Willow Run plant in Detroit, which made Chevrolet models until 2010, is now the site of the American Center for Mobility for self-driving research and testing.
- The auto supplier **Detroit Manufacturing Systems** hired nearly 400 workers at a new leased plant in Toledo to make Jeep Wrangler components and invested $70 million to equip and outfit it. In Detroit, the manufacturer invested $31.9 million to repurpose its existing facility with advanced machinery, robotics, and automation, as well as creating 225 high-tech jobs.

Youngstown in 2016, he promised to bring back jobs to the Factory Belt. "Don't sell your house, do not sell it," he said. "We're going to fill up those factories, or rip them down and build new ones. That's what's going to happen."

Voters believed him. But the reverse happened. GM continued to reduce work shifts as sales sagged. The Lordstown factory failed. And people felt the impact. Dave Green was president of UAW 1112 during the final shutdown of the Lordstown plant. Like many of his fellow workers, he took a transfer. He now works at a GM foundry a six-hour drive away in Bedford, Indiana, where he owns a condo. He returns to his Youngstown home for a long weekend every month. Green told me of his efforts to keep the Lordstown assembly plant open, including sending 10,000 Christmas cards and Valentine's cards to the GM CEO, with the message *Save my dad's job*. He told me he'd heard that Lordstown Motors would be paying a "decent wage of $20 an hour"—slightly more than new hires at GM. "I really hope that Lordstown Motors does well," he said. "The whole community has been impacted with high unemployment, poverty, and food lines."

In Youngstown I also met county commissioner David Young. He advised me to judge the city for myself and not to fall prey to stereotypes. "Youngstown has always been shorthand for economic despair in the national media," he observed. He recalled how an economist came through town and issued a death sentence based on the view that a brain drain had left the city with only the elderly, the impoverished, and workers with outdated skills. "He was so sure of his prognostication," Young said, then added, "I hope that our community might become part of an emerging market. The feeling in the community is, 'Oh no, not again. We have been promised this, and now it doesn't turn out to be true.'"

When I met Steve Burns at Lordstown Motors, he was full of EV optimism. Then he hit bumps in his road just as I did in his golf cart. Erik Gordon, a professor at the Stephen M. Ross School of Business at the University of Michigan and managing director at the student-run Wolverine Venture Fund, saw the problems before they happened: "It's one thing to do publicity stunts, tout preorders, build a prototype, and take it out on the test track. You have to look at the quality.

The question is whether Lordstown Motors can design and build a truck that will have the sufficient quality that fleet owners demand. [Burns] has to make sure there are no production delays. He needs the engineering and manufacturing to produce a vehicle that is going to be running all day on two delivery shifts, not parked next door." He was prescient. Especially when he said, "We'll have to see how reliable it is within the next few years." Other observers spoke of Burns's "hucksterish tones" and "phony cheerleading."

So it is important to be realistic. Industrial pioneers on the frontier can have a rough ride. While promising to bring in new technologies, talent, investment, and jobs for the future to rebuild remote areas, business challenges have led to stall-outs. Startups such as Lordstown Motors and PureCycle Technologies lean on strong corporate partners to climb. Sometimes they get a second chance, which could happen with Foxconn's ownership of the Lordstown plant. It isn't easy being at the forefront of such a major transition. Even in Silicon Valley most startups fail. But there are lessons to be learned with every failure, and a new generation of tech upstarts will look to these industrial models in the Midwest as a road map of what to do and what not to do. It only takes one breakthrough to start a new pattern of success. Otherwise, there is stagnation and the status quo, not the renaissance that the Rust Belt so needs.

Are the innovators there? Absolutely. Major players willing to take the risk to effect necessary change? A resounding yes. And as I saw on my trips through Ohio and neighboring states, there are plenty of venture capitalists willing to fund this important American renaissance. So the next stage of my heartland journey was to take a closer look at this world of venture capital and to explore how this insular financial industry is finally breaking out of the narrow confines of California's Silicon Valley and discovering its own backyard. Because major VC money from high-profile players is pouring into key heartland hubs. From Pittsburgh to Columbus, financiers are chasing deals for their portfolios, with the goal of creating a first-time crop of midwestern unicorns and startups.

Will it be enough to recapture the region's dominance?

PART TWO
The Money

Chapter Three

The Startup Investors

*How two Silicon Valley transplants launched a Columbus investment firm
and started piling up wins as the most impactful investor in the region*

At Drive Capital's sixth-floor office overlooking High Street in Columbus, it was hard to miss the firm's trademark truck parked next to the reception desk. How in the world did it get there? Did venture capitalist Mark Kvamme really drive it up a steep ramp and ace the landing inside, as he had boasted? Well, he did race sports cars on weekends and once suffered a serious injury in a crash. He's a risk-taker on the race track and on the venture capital trail, so I wouldn't put it past him. I asked Kvamme about it when we met. He laughed and showed me how the truck bed was sawed in two so it could be hoisted upstairs.

Columbus is a quick thirty-five miles from Lancaster over windy, hilly roads that soon turn to heavy traffic on the I-70 beltway. I'd driven there that morning, thinking of all the times I'd made this trip in the past. And now Columbus was booming, with its diverse population of close to a million, rebuilt neighborhoods, flock of tech startups, and well-educated millennials. The capital of Ohio, it had surpassed both Cincinnati and Cleveland in size and become the second largest city in the Midwest—and growing much faster than Chicago.

I talked with Kvamme about Columbus's resurgence when we went to lunch. He told me why he thinks the Midwest is America's next emerging market: abundance of knowledge-worker talent from Big 10 schools, 19 percent of the country's GDP, and patents. Columbus, he reminded me, is in close proximity to nearly half the US population as well as a large base of corporate customers and research institutions. He added one more factor everyone agrees on: a lower cost of living. Yet the Midwest has a scarcity of venture investment for startups, less than 10 percent of the nation's pot.

Kvamme was a true Silicon Valley player: a partner in Sequoia Capital, a board member at LinkedIn, and an Apple product manager. But he gave it all up to launch his own venture firm, Drive Capital, in Columbus. Going native, he even bought farmland in central Ohio, with cows, goats, and pigs. Skeptical colleagues in California thought he was crazy. But within a decade, Drive Capital had brought Silicon Valley success to the Midwest. With $1.2 billion and over sixty investments in game-changing startups, the Columbus-based firm applied Silicon Valley's well-crafted model of investing to the region. Drive Capital is within driving distance of most of the region's emerging tech hot spots and thousands of miles from Sand Hill Road's venture epicenter next to Stanford. Kvamme is proving the naysayers wrong.

In the early days of China's tech economy boom a few decades ago, I interviewed the country's pioneering venture-capital leaders. Little did I imagine their seedlings would grow into gigantic Chinese companies. Now, in my home region, here I was on a similar quest, talking to Mark Kvamme as part of my goal to assess the area's prospects of becoming a mini–Silicon Valley.

Midway into our lunchtime conversation, our server interrupted to ask if we'd like to order anything else. And plop—one of her earrings fell off and landed right on my plate. Well, that was the end of my meal, but my heartland upbringing told me not to make a fuss about it. Kvamme didn't seem bothered, and told the flustered server it was okay, not to worry. Not missing a beat, he said, "We're going to discover the next Larry Page of Google or the next Jack Dorsey of Twitter. Right here." He should know; he has long experience picking change-makers who can shape the tech future, and not just from his Silicon Valley pedigree. Before forming Drive Capital, he was Ohio's job-creation point person under governor John Kasich.

Drive Capital is well named—driving is the way to get around in the Midwest. The company has also shown drive in getting a head start in the region. Granted, there's no Apple, Alphabet, or Meta here. And hot spots like Austin and Miami seem more exciting than old Rust Belt lands. But having spent fifty years in Silicon Valley, watching it grow from its agricultural roots into the silicon age, Kvamme is convinced that technological transformation is coming from the consumer packaging, manufacturing, insurance, and healthcare companies of the Midwest. "This is the next frontier, where being close to the customer will be more important than being close to the technologist as we build the future technologies that have a great impact on our world," he said. And, as he confidently added, "Silicon Valley has been the center of tech, but you don't have to be there anymore. Entrepreneurs are building where they're strongest, and investors are finding them."

Within a year of our meeting, his firm scored two major wins with bets on Root, a Columbus-based technology company offering auto insurance; and Duolingo, the language-learning app developed in Pittsburgh. Root went public in October 2020 and soared to $6.7 billion in value, ranked in size right after California startups Airbnb, DoorDash, and Wish.[32] It was Ohio's first venture-backed, publicly traded company; its second unicorn; and Drive Capital's biggest performer so far. The firm's $67 million investment for a sizeable equity stake of 26.1 percent in Root skyrocketed to $1.46 billion at its trading debut. Then, Duolingo went public in mid-2021, valued at about $6.5 billion. Next up could be budding star Olive, a healthtech software company based in Columbus recently valued at $4 billion, a record-breaker for Ohio and high even by Silicon Valley standards.

The fear of missing out runs strong. Prominent VC firms from California, New York, and Boston have been keeping an eye on Drive Capital. They sense that now could be the time to capitalize on newly inspired entrepreneurs who are keeping the American dream alive in the heartland. It may take a while for a herd to arrive, but those at the front are a powerful bunch: big names in the VC world such as Ron Conway, PayPal cofounder Peter Thiel, Marc Andreessen, and Alan Patricof. Even investors from the Far East are poking around and doing deals.

Kvamme's cofounding partner, Chris Olsen, left a rising career at Sequoia Capital to gamble on this grand midwestern adventure. Now he's glad he did. Olsen told me how Kvamme pitched him on joining him as a partner and urged him to rethink his prejudices about the Midwest. "What are the odds we'd fail? But if we're right, then we have the opportunity to build multibillion companies and bring about an economic shift from the industrial revolution to the knowledge economy to technology. If you look at where the majority of the market cap is built by technology companies, it's no longer in Silicon Valley." Olsen sourced the firm's deal with Root, incubating the startup at Drive Capital's office. "It's impressive to achieve unicorn status, but becoming a public company is more challenging, even more challenging than starting it in Ohio," he said.

Olsen had tried to recruit Root's founder, first-time entrepreneur Alex Timm, to join the Drive team. Instead, Timm successfully pitched his business idea: a mobile-only platform that calculates insurance premiums by telematics, or data science tracking of driver habits, rather than conventional factors of age, gender, and credit history. Timm had spotted an opportunity to reinvent the outdated automotive-policy field while working at Nationwide Insurance after college.

Olsen is pleased with his move. And he knew the turf, having grown up in Cincinnati, a two-hour drive away. "Our fellow partners [at Sequoia] thought it was the dumbest thing ever, and crazy! I always thought that the quality of life would be higher in Silicon Valley than in Columbus, but I've found young, smart people here with good-quality ideas and the raw ingredients to build. There's a very positive environment in Columbus, and the cost of experimentation is low," he said.

Root, operating out of a slick new office building in sight of the state capitol, soon expanded across nearly two-thirds of the country, competing against legacy rivals like Progressive, Allstate, and GEICO. But in early 2022, Root laid off 330 employees or about 20 percent of its staff, citing increased costs and supply chain challenges due to the pandemic.[33] Chasing growth, Root is losing money—common among aggressive tech startups with a long runway. But remember—it took Amazon seven years to break even.

Shifting Sands

Since the 1990s, when Silicon Valley surpassed Boston's Route 128 as America's leading high-tech location, risk capital has been centered on Sand Hill Road in Menlo Park, California, the Wall Street of the West Coast. Here's where Sequoia Capital, Kleiner Perkins, and Accel helped to spawn Facebook, Google, Yahoo, Apple, and Oracle. Here's where web browser Netscape kicked off the dotcom boom and where its Iowa-born cofounder, Marc Andreessen, later formed Andreessen Horowitz, managing $28 billion in capital.

California has claimed nearly half of $322.8 billion in venture investments made nationwide, six of the ten largest VC funds, and six of the top-ten VC deals.[34] But the sands are shifting. The proportion of venture spending on Bay Area startups has shifted to below 30 percent for the first time in ten years, steadily declining from 40 percent in 2014.[35, 36]

The world's top innovation hub over the past half century—blessed with good weather, beautiful coasts, and access to leading universities—has fallen out of favor. Talented techies fed up with the high cost of living, congestion, wildfires, and the pandemic rented U-Hauls and packed up. Millennial talent fled to new boomtowns, many of them in the Midwest, where VC momentum had accelerated. Over the past decade, venture investment in twenty-five middle states nearly quadrupled to $20.2 billion and funded almost 18,000 startups in the heartland.[37] Startup investors in smaller inland hubs outside the coasts reached 3,700, up from 1,000 in 2011. Fundraising by VC firms beyond New York, California, and Boston picked up as well, to more than $21 billion from only $3 billion a decade ago.[38]

The money is also flowing from the coasts to the center. Over a hundred coastal venture funds seeded nearly 700 midwestern startups in five years, three times more than before.[39] Coming from California and New York, top firms such as Tiger Global, Google Ventures,

Sequoia Capital, Redpoint Ventures, and Scale Venture Partners added heft, deep pockets, and knowhow. Additionally, more than 200 angel investors[40] and over 300 accelerators and incubators have made investments in the Midwest[41]—alongside a number of government-supported venture development organizations.

The trend escalated as bigger VC funds[42] and more regional venture shops emerged in the Great Lakes states: High Alpha and Allos Venture in Indianapolis, Renaissance Venture Capital in Ann Arbor, Refinery Ventures in Cincinnati, and Hyde Park Angels in Chicago, among others. Previously, entrepreneurs in the industrialized Midwest had been limited to state government programs, Kickstarter campaigns, loans, pitch contests, incubators, accelerators, or the fallback—friends and family. Going to Silicon Valley to raise money was hopeless without connections.

Venture financing of promising heartland companies is gaining muscle. Unicorns—privately held venture-backed startups valued at more than $1 billion—have multiplied, including the self-driving tech innovator Argo AI in Pittsburgh, the AI-powered healthcare software provider Olive in Columbus, and the online bidding marketplace StockX in Detroit.[43] Other high-flying achievers with midwestern origins have gone public: Rivian began trading on Nasdaq in November 2021 in a blockbuster $86 billion market debut that netted the electric-vehicle maker nearly $12 billion, although in a highly competitive and volatile market (it has since slashed production forecasts and faced supply-chain challenges).

Prominent Silicon Valley tech companies have also swooped in to acquire cutting-edge companies in the Midwest—nearly 1400 over the last decade.[44] Salesforce bought ExactTarget in Indianapolis for $2.5 billion, and Cisco snapped up Duo Security in Ann Arbor for $2.35 billion.

All this investment and acquisition activity in the Midwest gave me context for my meeting with Mark Kvamme. It also helped to know about the man himself. He grew up in Sunnyvale and was as Silicon Valley as could be. He is the son of E. Floyd Kvamme, who was executive vice president for marketing and sales at Apple when it launched the Macintosh personal computer. By the time Mark was

Drive Capital: An Overview

Location: Columbus   **Launched:** 2013
Cofounders: Mark Kvamme, Chris Olsen
Funds: 6 totaling $2.2 billion   **Investments:** 60
Investment sectors: robotics, edtech, AI, healthcare, fintech, future of work, cybersecurity
Geographic focus: Priority on Columbus but broadly Midwest and extending into Canada
Notable backer: Ohio State University
Notable deals:

- **Physna:** search engine for 3D images
$6.9 million, 2019; $20 million coinvestment led by Sequoia Capital, January 2021; $56 million investment by Tiger Global with GV, July, 2021
- **Path Robotics:** AI-driven welding robot maker
led $12.5 million deal, 2018; $56 million coinvestments led by Addition with Basis Set Ventures, Lemnos Labs, May 2021; $100 million by Tiger Global with SVB, July 2021
- **Olive:** AI-powered healthcare bots for administrative tasks
$5 million, 2013; $15 Million, 2016; $106 million, September 2020; $225 million, December 2020; $400 million, 2021; coinvestors: Tiger Global, General Catalyst, SVB Capital, Khosla Ventures
- **Gecko Robotics:** wall-climbing industrial inspector
led $40 million investment 2019; coinvestors: Founders Fund, SoftBank, and billionaire entrepreneur and TV personality Mark Cuban
- **Finite State:** cybersecurity firm
$7 million seed, 2019; $12.5 million from Energy Impact, Zetta Venture Partners; $30 million, August 2021 with Schneider Electric Ventures, Merlin Ventures
- **Forge Biologics:** gene therapy startup
led $40 million, mid-2020; $120 million with life science investors, 2021
- **IPOs:** autotech insurer Root in Columbus, language learning app Duolingo in Pittsburgh
- **Acquisitions:** Yelp paid $40 million in 2017 for restaurant waitlist app NoWait, after a $10 million Drive-led deal in 2014; recreational-vehicle maker Thor snapped up digital road-trip planner Roadtrippers in 2018; event technology leader Cvent acquired Kapow for an undisclosed price in 2018; and Creative Solutions snagged Livestream's game livestreaming business in 2021 for $35.9 million

twenty, he had graduated from the University of California at Berkeley and was working at Apple. Soon after, he started his own company selling Apple software and hardware, but it went belly up within two years. Better luck came when he colaunched the interactive marketing agency CKS Partners, specializing in launching web-centric brands just as the dotcom boom was starting. The firm's clients included Yahoo, Amazon, and the ad campaign that brought Apple into the iPod era. CKS went public in 1995 and was sold in 1998 to USWeb in a stock swap of about $340 million. Kvamme joined Sequoia Capital in 1999, height of the tech bubble, and he told me that the budding venture scene in Columbus reminded him of the early dotcom days in Silicon Valley.

Kvamme got his life-changing initiation to Ohio in 2011, when then-governor Kasich offered him a cabinet post as the state's development director. He started jetting to Ohio, taking a salary of $1 for the public service job. After a lawsuit alleging that out-of-state residency made Kvamme ineligible for the post, Kasich appointed him to a policy role as interim chief investment officer and an architect of the nonprofit JobsOhio, set up to jump-start the Buckeye State's jobs growth. When JobsOhio was hit with political and legal roadblocks over its unique funding through state liquor license profits in October 2012, Kvamme resigned and made plans to return to the private sector. But his attachment to Ohio had grown. He had married a local woman, Megan Browning, a former investment banker, so he had an additional personal incentive to stay.

Kvamme's two years in a political power post gave him an up-close perspective on the Ohio's potential. Within a few months of resigning, he'd launched his own venture firm in Columbus. After pitching 230 potential supporters, he landed a sizeable $50 million capital commitment from Ohio State University for his first fund of $250 million. Over the following years, Drive Capital reloaded with more than two billion dollars to inject into expanding, mature tech companies. Satisfied with initial results, Ohio State University reinvested in these subsequent larger funds. The university's confidence was a good sign, signaling that more money from endowments, pension funds, and institutions were possible for Midwest venture capital funds.

Drive Capital's playbook from Silicon Valley was working in Middle America. In venture jargon, it was all about finding that *killer app* that solves a *pain point*, then pump it up with a bold business plan, ample funding, and an ownership stake, ensuring a return when the startup gets acquired or goes public. Oh . . . and then repeat that pattern.

Venture capital is a high-risk business. Only a few venture deals bring in off-the-chart financial returns, while many fail.[45] About two in ten portfolio companies don't survive past their first year.[46] To beat the odds, venture capitalists look for entrepreneurs with dreams of disrupting the status quo, solving the climate crisis, curing cancer, or doing more than tinkering in their garage. Their search is for the next new thing and to invest in it early before others catch on so they can reap the highest financial rewards.

Drive Capital created a buzz in Columbus. Young people mingle and exchange ideas at rooftop parties next door to its Short North office—like many I've been to in Silicon Valley. As the economy was reopening in mid-2021, the team held a "Summer Drive" party, billed as a "wonderful celebration of inoculation." Big on branding, the firm hosts an online show, "Ask Drive Anything," and publishes a newsletter, aptly named *U Turn*. Its website features a "startup IQ test" for founders and potential hires to find out if their personality, logic, and reasoning skills would fit in well in an entrepreneurial team.

Getting the green light from Drive Capital investors can put entrepreneurial founders on the fast track. Word is getting around that upstarts without backing from Drive won't get noticed by the big firms on the coasts. Yet being the early bird in the Rust Belt hasn't been easy for the venture firm. It has taken daring, time, energy, and patience. But Kvamme knows it can pay off to invest early in the right emerging region. Young startups that haven't been discovered yet can be invested in at a lower valuation. As they scale up, their value usually increases, until they go public or get merged or acquired.

The team leaders logged a lot of miles, combing university campuses and hearing hundreds of startup pitches. Heartland entrepreneurs are getting the hang of venture capital but need coaching. Midwestern entrepreneurs can get the job done, but they don't think big enough. There are few heroes to follow, unlike in Silicon Valley. Given this gap, it can pay for founder and investor to be in close range of each other. Out of Drive Capital's numerous investments in new tech businesses, about one-quarter are in Columbus. This is a technique borrowed from Sand Hill Road: clump startups within a thirty-mile radius. Several of the firm's startups have relocated to central Ohio. But Drive is not afraid to look a bit farther afield, within a six-hour drive or a short flight, and has invested in startups in Chicago, Pittsburgh, Ann Arbor, Minneapolis, and Toronto.

Billionaire Support

The innovation of the heartland has attracted the attention of not only the big venture capital firms from the coasts but also the interest of two of America's most successful entrepreneurs, Steve Case and former New York City mayor Michael Bloomberg. They have recognized the yawning economic divide between the coastal epicenters and rising midlands and are spearheading a push to bring Silicon Valley knowhow and capital to the Midwest. Having traversed the Rust Belt, they've written several checks for high-potential young businesses, though neither has set up shop in the heartland . . . yet. Roy Bahat, who heads Bloomberg Beta, an early-stage venture firm in San Francisco backed by Bloomberg, told me that he expects more and more venture money will flow into the Midwest from the usual hot spots as connections and familiarity with the heartland's revival increases.

Bloomberg's VC group has supported a series of "Comeback Cities" tours of the Rust Belt, which have brought more than a dozen venture capital investors from Silicon Valley and New York to Youngstown and Akron, Ohio; Detroit and Flint, Michigan; and South Bend, Indiana. The first tour, in 2018, sparked the launch of a $10 million microfund, Comeback Capital, for startups located outside traditional hubs. Headed by Case Western University professor Scott Shane, the fund has funneled money into more than forty tech startups, including Flint-based e-scooter and smart-charger Kuhmute. Additionally, Bloomberg Beta signed its first deal in Columbus, investing in Strongsuit, cofounded by former consultants at McKinsey and Boston Consulting, as a concierge service for busy professionals to unload to-do household tasks.

Patrick McKenna, an experienced entrepreneur and fund manager and a partner at Comeback Capital, has described the heartland as an emerging market—a bit more volatile than Silicon Valley but with lower prices and a potentially higher upside. Like others, McKenna also praised Drive Capital for treating "every company like it's in Silicon Valley."

Steve Case has also run tours in the Midwest, called the "Rise of the Rest," which have spotlighted overlooked startup hubs. There have been eight tours to more than forty cities, big red luxury buses roaring into Tulsa, Birmingham, and other inland cities. Following up, Case launched two seed funds totaling $300 million, backed by such veteran business leaders as Amazon's Jeff Bezos, KKR's Henry Kravis, LinkedIn's Reid Hoffman, eBay's Meg Whitman, and others. The money has gone into more than two hundred heartland startups, much of it through investments of $100,000 that Case and his team awarded to winners in pitch contests.

Case wants to level the playing field for entrepreneurs in every state, in every zip code. As he has pointed out, the majority of venture investment nationally goes to startups in three states—California, New York, and Massachusetts. "We can do better," he told me in an interview, adding that his seeding of startups in underserved areas is meant to build a model home for others to come look at and then add more. He has described a boomerang effect of talent and capital, which moved to Silicon Valley over the last half century but is starting to return, accelerated by the trend toward remote working and virtual meetings. "This could be the moment for interest in the rest [of the country]. These trends can accelerate entrepreneurship into a dispersed innovation economy. The brain drain to the coasts will slow a little," he predicted.

Inspired by Case and his Rise of the Rest agenda, *Hillbilly Elegy* author J. D. Vance formed a venture shop in Cincinnati to invest in tech startups in overlooked Appalachian areas struggling with hardship. His Narya Capital has $93 million in funds to invest, as his VC site reads, "in exceptional teams tackling scientifically complicated business challenges." I was surprised to see Vance and a small team of helpers carrying banners down Broad Street in my hometown's July 4 holiday parade in 2021—though perhaps I shouldn't have been, given his political aspirations.

Table B: The Gap in Venture Capital Investment in the US

State	Deals	Dollars
California	37% of Deals	49% of $
2021	5,342	$157,533.60
2020	3,948	$84,189
2019	3,063	$77,297.70
New York	14.8% of Deals	15.4% of $
2021	2,140	$49,634.70
2020	1,440	$18,152
2019	1,050	$14,311.79
Massachusetts	7.6% of Deals	11% of $
2021	1,096	$35,499.00
2020	850	$17,367
2019	660	$11,885.72
Michigan	1.1% of Deals	.4% of $
2021	162	$1,386.70
2020	147	$3,332.70
2019	140	$803
Illinois	2.9% of Deals	2.3% of $
2021	412	$7,316.70
2020	321	$2,588.40
2019	312	$2,213
Pennsylvania	2.7% of Deals	2.1% of $
2021	384	$6,721.70
2020	311	$2,137.30
2019	289	$2,653.10
Ohio	1.1% of Deals	.7% of $
2021	179	$2,351.40
2020	167	$1,450.30
2019	149	$960

Table B: The Gap in Venture Capital Investment in the US (cont.)

Indiana	1% of Deals	.2% of $
2021	143	$490.50
2020	125	$348.80
2019	145	$380.80
Kentucky	.3% of Deals	.06 of $
2021	50	$200.00
2020	45	$255.90
2019	35	$248.10
West Virginia	.07% of Deals	.01% of $
2021	10	$29.10
2020	3	$0.90
2019	1	$0.02
National	**Deals**	**Dollars**
2021	14,411	$322,800.00
2020	11,651	$164,000.00
2019	10,430	$133,421.50

Source: *National Venture Capital Yearbook*, 2020, 2021, 2022

Why the fuss over venture capital? Because this asset class has an outsized impact on job creation for its relatively small size.[47] Venture-funded startups in 2020 alone employed 4.4 million workers nationwide.[48] Five of the most valuable publicly traded companies in the United States were venture-funded, all on the West Coast: Apple, Microsoft, Amazon, Alphabet, and Facebook (Meta). The dominant West Coast firms that funded these tech titans are well entrenched. A capital shift to the Midwest will charge up regional tech startups across key businesses, from healthcare, insurance, and education to cybersecurity, transportation, and commerce. But let's be clear: Silicon Heartland won't replicate Silicon Valley. The midwestern pace is not as fast or as impactful as the Silicon Valley dotcom boom of the 1990s or the China tech pop a decade later. The Midwest's build-out is more gradual and—until recently—mostly beneath the radar.

It's important to be realistic about what the Midwest can expect to achieve from this VC interest. The massive venture-capital success of firms that invested in the deep-tech innovators of Silicon Valley and the giant Chinese companies that went public, like JD.com and Alibaba,[49] is unlikely to be matched in the Midwest. In the new heartland terrain, risks remain, including lack of confidence and less upside potential.

My own tour of the Midwest allowed me to explore these budding mini–Silicon Valleys. I learned that each market leverages its own anchor venture shops and specialized technologies. Pittsburgh is known for AI and robotics, with Draper Triangle as the leading investor in regional startups. Cleveland is rich in biotech, bolstered by several life science investors as well as the venture accelerator JumpStart. Indianapolis is a stronghold of B2B software services, thanks in part to the firm High Alpha.

The distance between these hubs is a disadvantage for the region as a whole. Innovation tends to compound within tight clusters. There is no focal point like Sand Hill Road's dominant string of venture shops next to the Stanford University campus. Columbus is the closest comparable, but it's about a three-hour drive from this central hub to other up-and-comers. Flights are not that frequent to San Francisco or New York and can be pricey. It's no wonder that Drive Capital's logo includes a graphic of a highway!

Nearly two hundred miles from Columbus, Pittsburgh has emerged as a favored fishing hole for venture investors, with AI, robotics, and other tech startups to catch. Drive Capital held a road show here in 2014, a newly raised $250 million fund as bait. Chris Olsen and other Drive colleagues came to Pittsburgh's Oakland innovation district, next to the Carnegie Mellon and University of Pittsburgh campuses, broadcasting the message that local entrepreneurs don't have to travel to Silicon Valley to get funding. They soon inked several investment deals with edgy local startups.

Duolingo emerged as their star. Drive Capital's initial $25 million outlay in 2017 paid off with an equity stake worth $183 million at its public market trading debut four years later. Coinvestors also profited from the IPO of the top-ranked language learning app: celebrity angel investor Ashton Kutcher, popular podcaster Tim Ferriss, as well as VC stalwarts Kleiner Perkins, NEA, Union Square Ventures, and General Atlantic. So did Google's Capital G, injecting $30 million in 2019 to make Duolingo the first unicorn-valued, venture-backed startup in Pittsburgh. Just months before it went public, the popular and engaging platform collected another $35 million from investors in a deal that valued this ten-year-old company at $2.4 billion.

This kind of buildup is rare in the Midwest and a reason why Drive Capital gets good reviews. "I love them. They are bringing their Silicon Valley style to the Midwest and have been very active in the region," Dave Mawhinney said to me. Dave is the executive director of the Swartz Center of Entrepreneurship at Carnegie Mellon University. He explained that Drive Capital "understands portfolio management, that two or three of their investments will return the fund. They are entrepreneurial friendly. Their terms sheets [on deals] are very clean. They don't try to limit the downsides with liquidation preferences [when a startup goes bust]. They bring entrepreneurs together in their portfolio to share info on scaling up."

Pittsburgh's Giant Shoulders

I drove to Pittsburgh to catch up with the city's longtime venture capital leader, Draper Triangle. As its name implies, the firm is linked to well-known startup investor Tim Draper, who described Draper Triangle as "awesome. They have been a catalyst to transform Pittsburgh. Lots of amazing companies that they seeded." Draper has backed quite a few winners, including Tesla, SpaceX, Hotmail, Skype, and Twitter. A billionaire bitcoin enthusiast and digital currency investor, he also runs the entrepreneur training school Draper University in San Mateo, California.

I met Draper Triangle's cofounder and general partner Jay Katarincic in their twentieth-floor suite at the Gateway Center in Pittsburgh. He informed me that Draper Triangle is winding down and not making any new investments. That wasn't great news for Pittsburgh, though he quickly told me about a new early-stage venture fund that is spinning off from Draper Triangle: a rebranded Magarac Ventures, which is raising a $150 million fund, surpassing the predecessor firm's last fund at $80 million. The name signifies heft. Joe Magarac, a Paul Bunyan–type folk hero, was known to Pittsburgh steelworkers for his storied shoulders as big as a steel mill door and hands like the huge ladles used to pour molten steel.

The Magarac partners are primed to take on this heavy lifting on their own after depending on the Draper name, connections, and support for over twenty years. Their breakaway comes at a pivotal time. "The Pittsburgh tech and venture ecosystem has been slowly emerging but is now in a position to explode," Katarincic told me. His partner Zach Malone, who had joined us, added, "There are a ton of exciting companies to invest in but not enough capital. There's a tremendous shortage. It's an opportunity for us, and we do welcome more funds to come in from Silicon Valley, where hot deals are chased by funds."

The partners recruited Will Allen, an angel investor and former player for the Pittsburgh Steelers, to join the firm. "Will and I are the only general partners under the age of fifty-five in the whole city," Malone pointed out. "He's opened doors for us in deal flow and investors. He's a great networker."

Magarac Ventures should help to fill the shallow pool in southwestern Pennsylvania: $3.6 billion in 182 businesses in 2021, and $10.5 billion in 600 regional startups over the past decade, including $2.6 billion from IPOs.[50] In an encouraging sign, as many as 42 VC firms worldwide (including the prominent firms SoftBank, Bessemer Venture Partners, Greycroft, Warburg Pincus, and General Atlantic) recently made their first investment in Pittsburgh.[51] More will surely follow their lead. After all, Pittsburgh has status for world-class technical capabilities, research, and tech talent.

"Draper Triangle has been very, very important to the Mid-Atlantic and Midwest region. They have a good track record," Dave Mawhinney told me. But he added, "We still do not have many resident venture capitalists. Most of the new money has come from outside investors." The few venture players in the Pittsburgh area are specialized, relatively small regional efforts, such as state-supported Innovation Works and its affiliated Riverfront Ventures.

In this funding desert, Draper Triangle had a distinct advantage. The partners typically heard as many as a thousand pitches yearly, only gave the okay to three, and amassed a solid track record: more than half of its portfolio companies have been acquired, including buys by Oracle and Medtronic. Seven of those startups returned ten times or better on the firm's initial investment. Venture capitalists know that it's not about hitting a home run every time. A few of its tech deals didn't make it.[52] (See appendix A.)

One standout has been Locomation. It's in a sweet spot for Pittsburgh tech: AI-powered self-driving vehicles. Locomation (a great name) is a semiautonomous driving technology for two-truck convoys, capitalized with more than $63 million in venture funding. With its patents, one long-haul driver keeps watch on the self-driving system, while a second can be off-shift in a follower vehicle. Then they can switch positions.

The company was founded in 2018 by brothers Cetin and Tekin Mericli, immigrants from Istanbul, who earned PhDs at Carnegie Mellon. The brothers obtained the first commercial order for an autonomous-driven truck from Wilson Logistics, to equip its 1,120 trucks. Cetin spoke to me from the road, where he was doing tests. "This purchase order is just the beginning of a significant leap toward autonomous technology for the entire trucking sector," he said. "We completed our first real-world commercial trial with flying colors, and we deliver commercial loads with our autonomous convoy on a daily basis. And our first delivery? During COVID?" He laughed as he told me, "A trailer full of toilet paper!"

SaaS Stars

My next stop was Indianapolis, a burgeoning venture hub in the core heartland that is making a mark with B2B software service startups. On my itinerary were meetings with two high-net-worth regional venture capitalists: Scott Dorsey at High Alpha and Don Aquilano, cofounder of Allos Ventures. Both firms, deeply rooted in the Hoosier culture, are focused on building up high-growth enterprise companies, mostly in Indianapolis. They've raised successive funds, and their impact has spawned a new generation of rising software-as-a-service (SaaS) stars, increasingly paired up with investors from Silicon Valley, Los Angeles, New York, Boston, and Hong Kong.

Dorsey, who moved to Indianapolis after earning his MBA from Northwestern University and a brief stint with Chicago-based internet incubator Divine InterVentures, shared that "the Indy startup scene is a mix of ideas and capital in a compelling way. We have examples of success stories but we need more heroes and more nudges to get a full potential level. We are starting to see some coastal VCs, but it has to be a hot enough company to get inbound investment."

High Alpha's venture studio resulted from Dorsey's success at ExactTarget, a digital marketing company formed in 2000 to help businesses start using the emerging medium of email for marketing and customer connections. The startup climbed to over $300 million in revenues, raised $161.5 million in 2012 on the New York Stock Exchange, and hit the jackpot in 2013 when it was acquired by Salesforce for $2.5 billion.

Dorsey pulled off this win by relying on strong bonds in Indiana's tech community. His mentor and lead angel investor was Bob Compton, who in 1988 planted investor seeds in Software Artistry, Indiana's first software company to go public and eventually acquired by IBM for $230 million. Software Artistry was founded by Don Brown, who has been a great practitioner of repeat entrepreneurship—an important skill in an emerging startup environment. An Indianapolis native, Brown sold three startups to IBM, GM, and Genesys Telecommunications Laboratories. "My approach," he told me, "is to hire only those who can develop your products—spend money on the engineers. You have to have a healthy sense of paranoia, like a street fight. Being better is the only way to stay in business."

Rounding out my regional tour of venture investors, I drove southeast and crossed the state line into West Virginia, where the hilly terrain inspired John Denver's classic "Take Me Home, Country Roads." As I drove, I recalled how I would get carsick on this winding route when our family drove across the state to visit the museums and sights of Washington, DC.

I was headed to Morgantown to meet Mike Green, who runs Mountain State Capital, an investor in Appalachian startups, including several in West Virginia, which ranks at the bottom nationally in venture capital investment: the state had ten startup financings in 2021, totaling $29 million.[53] Green has worked for Silicon Valley startups and is originally from New York, but he has found that the lifestyle in West Virginia suits him. "Lakes, mountains, good-quality air, and enjoyable lifestyle," he would tell me. "What was lacking was capital. I went on a mission to initiate a startup culture."

We met in the lobby of the Marriott Hotel next to the Monongahela River. We were joined by plastic surgeon Tom McClellan, inventor of Serucell, a skin-care serum that's formulated to eliminate wrinkles and sagging skin (Green is an investor in Serucell). A West Virginia native, McClellan trained at an affiliate of Harvard Medical School and at Tufts Medical School in Boston and holds thirty-five patents. "I wanted to have a big impact in a small place," he told me, explaining how he cofounded the Serucell Corporation lab and production facility in West Virginia. He showed me another of his breakthroughs, Fingy3D, a 3D-printed finger prosthetic that can be ordered online and costs less than fifty dollars. It was encouraging to meet with such exciting entrepreneurship in a state that really needs that kind of vision.

After my Morgantown meeting, I was back on the road and across the state line to Ohio, to the familiar turf of Athens and the Ohio University campus, where I connected with venture capitalist Bill Baumel, who had brought his twenty years of Silicon Valley credentials back to his home state in 2016 and made bets on innovative, disruptive companies from his university-supported, $40 million Ohio Innovation Fund. "There's no shortage of good startups in the state," he told me. "The challenge is finding CEOs who can grow big tech companies and encouraging founders to think big. In the last few years, we've seen the development of unicorns, billion-dollar acquisitions, and serial entrepreneurs who weren't here a few years ago."

He steered me to one of his star deals, Stirling Ultracold, which has gained national attention for its ultrachilly biomedical freezers that can store COVID-fighting vaccines for distribution. I was eager to check out this innovator, which I found on a backcountry road in the small town of The Plains. Baumel invested $10 million in the twelve-year-old business, which paid off in March 2021 with an all-stock acquisition valued at approximately $258 million by Nasdaq-listed, Seattle-based BioLife Solutions. This deal chalked up the largest venture-backed exit in southeastern Ohio and one of the biggest statewide.

I visited Stirling Ultracold just months before the acquisition, and CEO Dusty Tenney gave me a tour of its facility, with its highly focused worker force of 150, squeaky-clean environment, and patented freezers. The staff was hustling to keep up with demand from clients like Pfizer, Johnson & Johnson, and AstraZeneca. I was so impressed by this small, rural company heading for $100 million in revenues that I encouraged my brother to apply for a job there!

My VC tour had taken me through four states and convinced me that the funding required to fuel the comeback of the heartland was robust. As more venture capitalists follow Drive Capital's lead and put midwestern tech startups on the map, a tipping point is in sight. New companies in the Rust-Belt-turned-Tech-Belt are making their mark, attracting more investment, and triggering the additional capital required to support the entrepreneurial talent that is creating a Silicon heartland. I had seen the same narrative unfold in China twenty years ago, and my in-depth visit now convinced me that it could also work in my homeland, if not as quickly.

The venture pot is growing. But too few talents are willing to take a risk and go out on their own on what is always going to be an uncertain path. It may take a next cycle of business builders before this risk-taking mentality evolves and propels a rebalancing of the economic divide—between rich and poor, coasts and inlands—in the country.

But I was encouraged. And as my travels continued, I was further heartened by how this transformation of the Midwest was broadening in scope, as I learned of the rise of startups and investors led by people of color and those from other underrepresented communities who are more involved than ever in this progress. New financial commitments by socially conscious investors into venture shops and startups are changing the long-dominant white, male Silicon Valley club. Locations hardest hit by the economic meltdown of prior decades are getting entrepreneurial attention. This trend promises to have major impact in putting the Rust Belt in the forefront once again, in a new way.

Chapter Four

Black Ventures Matter

How innovative VC firms are driving the funding
of diversity-focused startups in the heartland

Today, opportunities for startups led by people of color, outside the typically white Silicon Valley boys' club, are beginning to open up. A select group of venture capitalists is investing in midwestern small businesses founded by underrepresented communities. Their trailblazing path comes at a time when the nation confronts lingering diversity and racial inequality issues.

My journey throughout the old Rust Belt cities exposed me to plenty of evidence of social unrest: boarded-up storefronts, broken windows, trashed sidewalks, and barren streets. More than half a century after the passage of the Civil Rights Act, substantial economic differences between whites and African Americans continue to be a source of social and political tension. Black Lives Matter protests had rocked many midwestern cities, including Detroit and Cincinnati, and I was keen to see how investors were doing their part in helping to address the complex issues that lay at the root of the tensions that led to the protests.

After visiting my family in Lancaster over the July 4 holiday (no parade or fireworks because of COVID restrictions), I drove the two-hour route to Cincinnati. I knew the city well—in my younger years I had a boyfriend there, and we used to enjoy riding the roller coaster at King's Island Amusement Park. The roller coaster is still there in this riverside community, which flowered during the Gilded Age, when it was called Queen City, a creative and economic hub during America's westward expansion.

Cincy—as it's known today—was a major stop on my road trip to explore old manufacturing and mining centers now prospering in a new digital economy. For my trip to this city built on seven hills, I stayed at a hotel in the peaceful hilltop oasis of Lytle Park, next to the landmark Taft Museum of Art. My room overlooked an expressway and the Ohio River and was within walking distance of the Great American Ballpark, home stadium for the Cincinnati Reds. In the morning I drove to Avondale, a multicultural, developing neighborhood that has struggled with high crime, economic decline, and racial strife dating back to the 1960s riots during the civil rights movement. More recently, Black Lives Matter rallies demanding justice for victims of police shootings have made headlines there.

I drove to the University of Cincinnati's recently opened 1819 Innovation Hub, named for the university's founding year. This four-story space, previously a vacant Sears department store, was remade for $38 million into a center for discovery. It's well outfitted with a venture accelerator; engineering lab; coworking areas; conference rooms; and office spaces for seed capital investor CincyTech, a Kroger innovation lab, and a Procter & Gamble simulation and research base.

During the tumultuous summer of 2020, when protests against racism and police brutality raged coast to coast, several investment firms launched new funds aimed at supporting diverse entrepreneurs. A number of socially conscious investors were likely prospects as sources of capital, such as Melinda Gates, through her transformational Pivotal Ventures, and oil executive George Kaiser, via his Tulsa-based family foundation. Investors began putting the money to work right away in tech startups founded by underrepresented entrepreneurs in the heartland. This unconventional focus will help to recharge the Midwest, especially in old-line Rust Belt cities that have majority African American populations and which have been historically underfunded.

Among the enlightened were several strategic investors, including SoftBank, Amazon, and Steve Case's Revolution. They took stock of their support of marginalized communities and upped their spending as a way of helping to end deeply ingrained social injustices. "We need to level the playing field and back greater entrepreneurship of people with different backgrounds and different places and spur job economic growth across the nation," Case has said. A staunch advocate of racial and gender equity, his portfolio favors diverse and women founders at 41 percent of his total investments.

These efforts are sorely needed in a tech and venture capital world that has been biased toward whites, males, and the coastal elite. Of all venture funding nationwide, Black and Latinx founders get only a tiny 2.6 percent, and the needle hasn't moved much since 2015.[54] Most venture firms don't have a single Black investor. Only a small percentage of startups have Black or Latinx executives.[55]

Owning your own business is a critical necessity for members of underprivileged communities. Given the significant hurdles in raising venture capital, many people instead turn to loans from family or friends, side jobs, and credit cards.[56] Black founders rarely raise external capital, and when they do it's comparatively small amounts.[57] Fellowships, internships, and leadership development programs such as HBCU.vc at historically Black colleges and universities seek to close these gaps, but more is needed.

Black Isn't a Niche

It's not as if there isn't a tradition of Black entrepreneurship. Robert L. Johnson, the founder of Black Entertainment Television, became the first African American billionaire. Yet they are severely underrepresented. Out of 2,755 billionaires worldwide, there are only thirteen who identify as Black, seven of those in the United States.[58] Most come from the world of sports and entertainment—Kanye West and Jay-Z, Michael Jordan, Tyler Perry and Oprah Winfrey, America's first Black woman billionaire. In the tech field, there have been two: David Steward, chairman of the largest Black-owned company in the country, World Wide Technology in St. Louis; and the philanthropist Robert F. Smith, CEO of the private equity firm and tech investor

Vista Equity Partners, who paid off student debt for nearly 400 recent graduates of Morehouse College.

Morgan DeBaun, founder of digital media company Blavity,[59] and Joy Buolamwini, creator of the Algorithmic Justice League, which identifies bias in artificial intelligence,[60] are important players in high tech. Neither has significant VC funding behind their work, however. Others raising money—and awareness—include LeBron James, who raised $100 million in 2020 for his video production startup SpringHill Entertainment, named after his childhood home in an Akron apartment complex.

A groundbreaking research study, digitalundivided's Project Diane, pointed out that less than 1 percent of total VC investment goes to Black and Latina founders. Today, women of color are starting businesses at an unprecedented rate and account for almost half of all women-owned enterprises.[61] Meanwhile, the gates have opened for female-led startups, with $20 billion and 2,669 deals since the prior decade.[62]

Cintrifuse's CEO, Pete Blackshaw, had this to say: "The Black Lives Matter movement has been a driver of innovation in Cincinnati. It's put this issue on steroids and created a sense of urgency." Other capital has come from the rebuilding cities of Detroit and Tulsa. The George Kaiser Family Foundation, which has committed $50 million to transform Tulsa into a tech hub and revive Black Wall Street (site of a horrible massacre in 1921), has earmarked funding to increase local job opportunities and entrepreneurial resources.

Ed Zimmerman, a venture tech lawyer at the New York–based firm Lowenstein Sandler and a cofounder with Theresia Gouw of First Close Partners, advises underrepresented managers on raising initial funds. Zimmerman, whose social and political views have influenced his work toward eradicating bias in venture capital, has invested in several Black-owned VC firms, including 645 Ventures and Harlem Capital in New York and MaC Venture Capital in Los Angeles. As Zimmerman has put it, "Investing in undervalued and overlooked funds is value investing."

Several other funds are helping startups increase their chances of breaking through the historical barriers. Diversity-focused initiatives by mainstream investors and corporations are creating a future that's more inclusive and equitable. (See sidebar on page 82.) But the gap in venture spending remains wide. Where money isn't available or doesn't seem the perfect solution, alternative resources can help to right things for marginalized entrepreneurs.

While in Cincinnati I also visited Mortar, an entrepreneurship hub that provides mentors to help low-income urban entrepreneurs build and run their startups. This program has offered hundreds of potential entrepreneurs a fifteen-week training academy and access to investor networks. The hub also runs a pop-up shop featuring its graduates' creations in the neighborhood of Walnut Hills, where there is a rich heritage of Black-run businesses, including Esoteric Brewing Company, a Mortar trainee.

Goalposts

From Cincinnati I moved on to Pittsburgh to meet several African American venture capitalists and entrepreneurs who are making a difference. I started with Ohio native Will Allen, a former safety for twelve years with the Pittsburgh Steelers and Tampa Bay Buccaneers who had been shaking things up in the venture world as an angel investor and partner in Magarac Ventures.

Allen got the VC bug when he visited Silicon Valley and attended a Bridge Summit hosted by Buccaneers teammate and Next Play Capital cofounder Ryan Nece, who manages $215 million across three funds and coinvestments in several well-known tech companies, including ByteDance, Peloton, and Impossible Foods. The Silicon Valley trip and Nece's success motivated Allen to try his hand at investing in real estate, energy, and tech.

In 2016, Allen cofounded the private equity firm Nascent Group Holdings in Columbus to invest in the Rust Belt. He followed through with an investment in Gravity Project, a mixed-use complex in Columbus's emerging Franklinton community, as well as several promising tech startups. He also advised LED lighting company Luna Energy Partners in Pittsburgh. His Will Allen Foundation, which advocates for education, equality, and civic responsibility, teamed up with Carnegie Mellon Robotics Academy to support a specialized technical training

New Funds for Underrepresented Entrepreneurs

- Large tech investor SoftBank rolled out its $100 million Opportunity Growth Fund to back fourteen startups led by entrepreneurs of color.
- Startup champion Steve Case held a three-day event during 2020 to support Black-founded startups outside the usual meccas. A pitch contest with judges from venture firms Foundry Group, First Round Capital, and Upfront Ventures was held with partners 100 Black Angels & Allies, Opportunity Hub, and Morgan Stanley's Multicultural Innovation Lab. Three winning teams were awarded a total of $2 million.
- Amazon launched the Black Business Accelerator, a $150 million, four-year commitment to support Black business owners with access to capital, mentorship, and marketing resources.
- Andreessen Horowitz formed a venture philanthropic fund, Talent x Opportunity Fund, with $2.2 million and matching contributions up to $5 million to seed upstarts and train entrepreneurs who lack the background, resources, and network to fast-track.
- The Bank of America, PayPal, Apple, Microsoft, Salesforce, MasterCard, Google, and Goldman Sachs opened their corporate coffers for investments focused on promoting racial equity.
- Additionally, a handful of smaller venture firms popped up across the country and loaded new funds dedicated to startups led by those traditionally underrepresented.
- Harlem Capital raised a second fund of $134 million in March 2021 with contributions from Apple and PayPal after an inaugural $40 million effort in December 2019 from 55 limited partners, including the State of Michigan Retirement Systems and the W. K. Kellogg Foundation.
- Elevate Capital launched a $40 million fund to invest in startups led by Black founders, anchored by Portland-based foundation Meyer Memorial Trust.
- The Fearless Fund, led by founding partner Arian Simone, started a $25 million fund in Atlanta to invest exclusively in early-stage businesses run by women of color.
- MaC Venture Capital, a majority Black-led investment firm in Los Angeles, raised an inaugural $110 million to double down on supporting overlooked young tech businesses on the brink of disruption, with participation from Foot Locker, Goldman Sachs, Bank of America, and other major corporates.

- Slauson & Co. debuted a $50 million fund in Los Angeles with backing from PayPal, Ashton Kutcher, and others, with veteran technology investor Ron Conway as an adviser.
- Backstage Capital in Los Angeles, focusing on funding startups run by people of color, women, and the LGBTQ community, is raising a $30 million fund after previous efforts in recent years. The founder, Arlan Hamilton, also had opened four accelerators, including one in Detroit.
- Black Tech Nation Ventures in Pittsburgh has launched a new fund with a mission to invest $50 million in Black-led startups.
- Main Street Ventures launched grant funding for the 4,000-member network Black Achievers in the tri-state region of Greater Cincinnati.
- Overlooked Ventures, based out of Columbus, is raising a $50 million fund with an initial commitment from Bank of America for startup founders who aren't white men.

course at a high school in Clairton, an impoverished town fifteen miles south of Pittsburgh and the home of Clairton Coke Works, the nation's only remaining coke-producing plant supplying iron and steel. Of twenty-two students who attended these training modules, seventeen earned a certificate that could open new employment opportunities or at least get them excited about a career in STEM.

Allen's work with his foundation is driven by personal experience. "I didn't have this kind of opportunity growing up. Sports was my only outlet," he told me. He grew up in Dayton, played football at Ohio State, and had a successful NFL career. He acknowledged that he had no idea how to enter the VC investing world until his former teammate Nece opened his eyes to the prospects.

Another Pittsburgh success story is the software developer Jim Gibbs, who talked to me about the challenges Black entrepreneurs can face. Up until recently, he had to bootstrap his startup, Meter-Feeder, an innovative app that does for parking what EZ Pass does for tolls, eliminating the hassle of inserting coins and checking time on the meter.

"Four dollars an hour at a parking meter is a lot of quarters, but with us, no one ever gets a parking ticket," Gibbs told me.

MeterFeeder has won contracts from commercial parking operators, fleets, and municipalities. Once smart cities and automated vehicles become more common, the app is well positioned to benefit, offering an easy way to pay to park.

To keep costs down, Gibbs's team of four developers works in a ground-floor office of a historic downtown building that is undergoing renovation in the impoverished, transitioning steel town of Braddock. Gibbs told me that, as a young boy growing up on Long Island, he was interested enough in computers that his parents sent him to a summer camp to learn software development skills. After attending Carnegie Mellon's School of Computer Science and working at *USA Today* and American Eagle, Gibbs became his own boss. "If I wasn't coding then, I was break-dancing. I was more spry then," said Gibbs, who has five young sons.

His first startup, in the late 1990s, was a mobile app for doctors to distribute healthy diet info. Ahead of the rise in smartphone popularity, it didn't take off. Then he cofounded MeterFeeder. Relying on his pitching and coding skills, he won several contests, including $10,000 through a California hackathon competition and $125,000 when he was accepted into a rigorous, three-month YCombinator startup accelerator program.

Eager to tap Sand Hill Road money, Gibbs traveled to Silicon Valley and spent four months hustling. Rejected, he headed home to Pittsburgh, where he knew people and could tap into connections. "We have built amazing technology, but folks would second-guess us. Black entrepreneurs can get a raw deal. I'm willing to do what I can to right this ship," he said, adding that he doesn't like "the idea of forced inclusion," or supporting entrepreneurs just to fill a quota. He's active in the community; on the board of Black Tech Nation, a Pittsburgh networking organization for entrepreneurs; and he keeps track of what's happening through a WhatsApp group of entrepreneurs of color.

These connections have helped to keep his business charged up. A number of African American investors, including Charles Hudson, founder of Precursor Ventures in Silicon Valley, serial tech entrepreneur Luke Cooper, and the VC fund Black Founders Matter, have all supported Gibbs. Word has gotten around about his startup's lean operation and smart technology, including nifty features such as a pay-by-car option where your vehicle automatically pays the meter when you turn off the engine, and a mobile device for traffic officers to issue tickets using an on-the-go printer. Additional capital up to $2.6 million flowed in from regional investors Mountain State Capital and Innovation Works, as well as from impact investment firm Segal Ventures.

The money Gibbs had raised for MeterFeeder, he told me, was enough to last "two years of burn"—cash to run the business. He wasn't looking for more unless other investors came calling, but he was happy that his small cofounding team still owned the majority of the startup's shares, a situation almost unheard of in Silicon Valley. "Pittsburgh is the perfect place to keep burn down while finding product fit. Costs are low, with a ton of smart people around. I'm here for the AI, and I stayed for the rent," Gibbs said. He was paying $650 for an 800-square-foot space—about a third of what he would have had to pay in the Bay Area.

It's refreshing to see investors and founders finding ways around conventions. Trying harder and looking for the path forward is a trait of most midwesterner entrepreneurs, particularly those from marginalized communities who can feel out of the loop or disadvantaged. Equality and diversity are becoming more and more important in the heartland's venture and tech scene. An increase in racial diversification across many predominantly white cities in the Midwest is bringing in a spark of spontaneity and creativity, beyond a small circle of elite folks who attended church, clubhouses, or university together. As this trend accelerates, a more open exchange of ideas in what was a rather bland, look-alike part of the business world becomes possible. Entrepreneurs and investors of color are powering up the investing universe. Though starting from a small base, these founders and investors are bigger factors in the region's transformation into the tech mainstream.

Part Three

Champions and Heroes

Chapter Five

Tech Icons to the Rescue

How tech icons are sparking entrepreneurship in Appalachia by gifting their time and millions of dollars for scholarships, career centers, innovation hubs, and business and engineering schools

Huntington and Morgantown are a three-hour drive apart. These West Virginia towns are the home to Marshall University and West Virginia University, respectively, two college campuses where West Coast high tech meets the Mountain State. Via these institutions, and in other ways, three tech icons from Silicon Valley—John Chambers, Brad Smith, and Ray Lane—are giving back to the place that shaped their values and exceptional careers. All three have contributed to Appalachia's renewal by encouraging entrepreneurship and funding breakthrough advancements.

This is country I'm familiar with. My family could pick up the Huntington radio signal from my childhood home in Jackson, Ohio, and the hills, valleys, and rivers of this region make me feel at home. So when I traveled to these towns to explore how these tech icons are helping to revitalize the region, I put the car on cruise control and simply enjoyed the heavenly mountainous scenery. But I was also conscious of the tough times people of this area have endured, and I looked forward to seeing what a difference champions like Chambers, Smith, and Lane can make in impoverished coal country dealing with deep and troubling socioeconomic issues. Their crusading efforts are planting seeds to motivate more self-starters and create jobs for a digital age.

Huntington is the state's second-largest city, though it has lost nearly half its population from a peak of 86,350 in 1950, as young, ambitious people moved on and steel and manufacturing industries declined. Marshall University is a town anchor with its 13,300 students. Morgantown also has a large student population—29,000—who attend WVU. Both universities are poised to help fix the state's ills by emphasizing new paths through entrepreneurship. They are ushering in change through scholarships, mentorship, incubators, R&D labs, and collaborative work spaces. They are encouraging a startup mentality by studies that combine engineering, computer science, and entrepreneurship. These programs have been so well supported by our trio of tech icons that all three have had buildings named after them at their alma maters—Smith at Marshall, and Chambers and Lane at West Virginia.

Their goal has been to import a Silicon Valley culture into this rural, scenic area. Brad Smith has described it as "dreaming the art of the possible, being willing to take risks, and recognizing that success and failure are equally the same, and simply an opportunity to learn. So there's no fear of failure, and this creates this sort of gestalt at Silicon Valley that becomes very contagious. It's an ecosystem that reinforces itself that attracts great talent and produces great ideas that venture capitalists want to invest in."

Brain, Heart, and Soul

Smith, former CEO of the $54 billion software business Intuit, had promised his mother he would come home to West Virginia. He did so in 2021 when he became president of Marshall University. It was part of a journey he'd begun three years earlier, when he stepped down as CEO of Intuit and, with his wife, Alys, an attorney from Ohio, cofounded the Wing 2 Wing Foundation, set up to advance entrepreneurship and education in overlooked and underserved regions in Appalachia. The couple contributed $60 million to Marshall University and started an initiative to entice remote workers to relocate to West Virginia.

I had interviewed Smith on my online show and asked him how West Virginia had shaped his success. "Well, it's completely responsible for anything and everything I've ever been able to achieve. It's the house that built me," he replied. "If you had to put a bow around how West Virginia shaped me, it taught me that life is a team sport and we're all angels who have one wing, and we can fly by holding on to one another. It taught me that intelligence is simply applied effort, and if you work hard, good things will happen."

Smith grew up in the Ohio River town of Kenova (named after the abutting states of Kentucky, Ohio, and Virginia). His upbringing there taught him "to lean into the things that scared me the most and, most importantly, to be a champion for the overlooked and underserved. And that is West Virginia, and everything I try to do every day."

He shared with me several formative moments from his childhood, including a story that helps explain his feeling about his home state. When he was six years old, he was watching television with his brothers when "suddenly, scrolling across the screen was a news alert about a plane crash in the Huntington tri-state area about a mile and a half away from my little hometown. I ran and looked out the window; the sky was glowing red and we could hear the sirens. My cousins, who were volunteer firemen, rushed to the scene. That was the Marshall University plane crash that killed the football team and many of our most pronounced citizens—a tragedy that was documented in the movie *We Are Marshall*, starring Matthew McConaughey. It devastated the entire community, but we were able to persevere and rebuild. I came out of this at that early stage of my life recognizing the importance of community and about working together to achieve things. It taught me an important lesson that life is a team sport."

Smith was considered the "Mr. Rogers" of Silicon Valley, a nice guy who was not ashamed to admit that he was homesick every day for West Virginia and never took off his class ring from Marshall. "It reminds me how I got here and what I have to do to help others." In Menlo Park, Smith would rise at 5:30 a.m. for an intense CrossFit workout. Now? He also can go hiking and rafting in the Appalachian Mountains.

I strolled around the Marshall campus and stopped to admire a statue of the university's namesake, Supreme Court chief justice John Marshall, which sits across from the Brad D. Smith Foundation Hall. This complex, renamed after Smith made several of what he calls pay-it-forward donations, houses an alumni center, conference space, and offices. Smith's gifts of $35 million to the university provided college scholarships for students from impoverished zip codes in the Appalachian region and funded a facility for the Brad D. Smith Center for Business and Innovation, with plans for opening to students in spring 2024.

The business school is being reframed with an entrepreneurial bent, and its centerpiece is the Impact Center for Entrepreneurship and Business Innovation (iCenter). The university provost, Avi Mukherjee, led me on a tour of the campus. "We are aiming to bring in Silicon Valley teaching to spur an economic revival through entrepreneurship and develop a creative mind-set," he explained. The iCenter supports entrepreneurs in residence, provides one-on-one coaching, holds workshops and business plan competitions, and showcases innovations through online pop-ups hosted by Intuit—and has recently expanded to work with high school students in vocational studies.

I also met several budding entrepreneurs, including Kelly Leonard, a Marshall MBA student and graduate assistant at the iCenter. She gained entrepreneurial experience here after her startup idea to help solve student debt won a competition with a $5,000 prize and a trip to Silicon Valley, where she attended a workshop at Intuit. "The feedback I got is that you need to know your *why*—and I'm still struggling with that," she told me. The next morning, Marshall University's then president, Jerome Gilbert, showed me around the ground-floor space of the downtown Visual Arts Center, which houses the Brad D. Smith Business Incubator. A converted department store, it is now an office and conference space for entrepreneurs. One of the new tenants is Justin Jarrell, a cofounder of North American Consulting Services, which does cybersecurity contracting work for the Department of Defense and has hired four interns from Marshall.

My Marshall visit was a great lesson in how focused, intelligent, and passionate philanthropy can expand entrepreneurial possibilities for a region that desperately needs innovation, and how the institutions established by that philanthropy can not only nurture new entrepreneurs but attract existing vibrant businesses into its orbit—paying it forward in a continuing cycle of success.

Mountaineering Spirit

From Huntington I moved on to Morgantown and WVU, alma mater of John Chambers, whom I'd also interviewed on my online show. I'd asked how his career had been shaped by growing up in a small town in West Virginia, and he immediately responded. "Many people might think Appalachia is a very poor section of the country and that I had a lot of challenges growing up. Actually, we were the chemical center of the world with FMC, DuPont, and Union Carbide in a town of 75,000, with 6,000 of the best engineers in the world. We were the coal-mining center of the world and had 25,000 coal miners. We had more millionaires in West Virginia than existed in the whole UK, and we were on top."

Whether or not this vibrant industrial background was a factor in shaping Chambers's business sense, he would go on to lead tech giant Cisco as it became a $47 billion corporate giant, acquiring 180 companies, turning more than 10,000 employees into stock-option millionaires, and becoming the backbone of the internet. Chambers spoke to me several times from his work space at his so-called Crow's Nest hideaway in the Bay Area foothills. "My parents taught me to appreciate the region and understand the values that also have shaped a large part of my values in life," he said. "I often say that if you ever broke down in a car driving anywhere in the world, and you had to walk up to a strange house in a remote location and ask for help, you would want it to be in West Virginia because of the quality of our people and the underlying fabric that they have."

Chambers stepped down as Cisco CEO in 2015 after two decades, but he wasn't about to retire. He went on to spearhead several initiatives to move his home state into a brighter economic future, including a high-speed transport system and a startup incubator on the WVU campus. He also made a substantial donation to the university aimed at spurring entrepreneurship and formed JC2 Ventures, which invests in disruptive tech startups.

"My parents taught me to watch trends. West Virginia began to fall from grace because we kept doing the right thing for too long," he said. "You need to stay ahead of market transitions, to disrupt or be disrupted. Because West Virginia didn't change, we got left behind. I realized that you've got to have the courage to change, that government and business and citizens have to work together to change."

Through Chambers's considerable influence, as well as statewide governmental and university effort, West Virginia has been selected to become the Virgin Group's testing and certification site for its high-speed transit technology called Hyperloop, although this project's future was unclear after company layoffs, a delayed construction start date, and a shift in focus to cargo transport. Located at an 800-acre former coal mine site near Mount Storm, Hyperloop's $500 million validation center could have a statewide economic impact of $48 million annually, generate thousands of manufacturing and construction jobs, and result in thousands of permanent employees, including 150 to 200 engineers. Up for federal funding to get back on track, the goal has been to create a high-speed transit system by 2039 that could connect Chicago, Cleveland, and Pittsburgh so that it would take less than a hour to travel between cities.

"Virgin Hyperloop had seventeen other states competing for this and we won," Chambers told me. "The reason we won is very simple. We understand building railroads and highways. We understand mechanical engineering challenges in one of the most mountainous parts of our country. Because we were a coal-mining area, we have access to many of the rare minerals that you need. We were able to mobilize the whole state to go after this, and we went from not even being on the radar to beating out states like Texas and others that went after this. It was the whole state and all the leaders putting aside their differences and focusing on what was the right outcome we want. It's one example of becoming a startup state right now by looking forward, not backward."

As I walked the river trail of the revitalized Wharf District of Morgantown, I came across construction of Reynolds Hall, a waterfront building to house the John Chambers College of Business and Economics. The hall doubles the space for a growing enrollment of business students and adds state-of-the-art technology and collaborative work spaces. Chambers also is working toward boosting West Virginia's economic prospects by establishing a venture capital fund for startups and creating a Center for Artificial Intelligence Management on campus.

"We've got to have the courage to become a startup state," Chambers said. It is a message he has been broadcasting globally—he is an adviser to government leaders in India and France on innovation agendas. "We've got to encourage entrepreneurship so people can get jobs, and we need to focus on outcomes."

As Chambers and other West Virginia boosters explored the potential of the expanded business school, they also created Vantage Ventures, an on-campus coworking and incubator space for entrepreneurs to pursue out-of-the-box tech ideas. Chambers shared his vision for the state's future at the center's grand opening, when he shared the stage with senators Joe Manchin and Shelley Moore Capito; WVU president Gordon Gee; and Chad Prather, president of Huntington National Bank.

Sarah Biller, Vantage Ventures' executive director, has described its mission: "Our first job is to provide a place and process for West Virginia entrepreneurs to launch high-impact, scalable business. We want them to access the same knowledge, resources, and capital that their peers have in cities like Boston, New York, and San Francisco." Biller is herself a graduate of WVU, a cofounder of the Boston nonprofit Fintech Sandbox, and a former manager of innovation ventures at the financial services giant State Street. She's a driving force of the state's push to attract fintech innovators.

Biller introduced me to several Vantage Ventures tenants, including two graduates of WVU's School of Engineering who are role models for the state's renewal. Kyle Gillis and James Carnes are cofounders of the startup Iconic Air, which uses AI and machine learning to monitor and analyze emissions data for the oil and gas industry. Iconic Air has leveraged their Vantage Ventures base to win a fifteen-month contract from the US Air Force and $135,000 funding from the West Virginia–based Country Roads Angel Network.

In Morgantown, I also learned more about efforts by venture capitalist Ray Lane, another WVU graduate who is best known for his remarkable turnaround of Oracle in the 1990s, when the enterprise software company's revenues grew from $1 billion to $10 billion in eight years. As part of his long venture capital career in Silicon Valley, Lane has been encouraging the next generation of West Virginians to pursue careers in STEM (science, technology, engineering, and math), including making a donation of $5 million to WVU to establish the Lane Department of Computer Science and Electrical Engineering. "Since I attended West Virginia University, I fell in love with the state, fell in love with the people, and fell in love with the university. I've stayed connected for a long time," Lane told me.

The new department includes the Lane Innovation Hub, a well-outfitted, spacious center for work on prototypes and advanced manufacturing. "The lab we've created is dedicated to each department within the College of Engineering," Lane explained. "So mechanical, aerospace, and computer engineering all have their own lab. Our great hope is that it's used not just by engineering students but by the whole university, as well as high school students in the state, and that this exposure changes their life and makes them think about being an engineer or using advanced tools like this."

Stimulating the Brain—and the Economy

These three influential leaders—Smith, Chambers, and Lane—also work together, regularly exchanging ideas and working on projects to improve the state's shockingly poor socioeconomic indicators. Together, they're funding groundbreaking research from one of West Virginia's best-kept tech secrets: the WVU Rockefeller Neuroscience Institute (RNI), founded by former senator and governor John D. "Jay" Rockefeller IV, who had seen his mother suffer from Alzheimer's disease.

At RNI I met the renowned neurosurgeon Ali Rezai, who leads the institute and its thousand faculty members, medical practitioners, researchers, and support staff. Linked to the state's largest health system, WVU Medicine, the institute employs about as many as once worked in the coal mines. As I walked into the lobby of RNI's Innovation Center, I passed by a huge mural that depicts half a million neurons in the human brain. I marveled as I listened to Dr. Rezai describe his breakthrough work in brain stimulation and focused ultrasound to treat Parkinson's, chronic pain, drug addiction, traumatic brain injuries, anxiety disorders, and dementia. Rezai holds sixty patents and is applying what he calls rapid cycle innovation to advance his technology. He said he expects soon to have one spin-out from his work that is "ripe for venture capital."

That product is a wearable health-tracking device and smartphone app that leverages AI to predict viral infections such as COVID three days before the onset of symptoms. The app connects with a wedding band–like tracker made by Oura Health in Finland to monitor changes in circadian rhythms, heart rate, and body temperature—what Dr. Rezai described as a "human operating system." The Rockefeller institute is deep-mining the data points to gain more insights about chronic pain, addiction, and other illnesses. Chambers, Smith, and Lane have already invested $1.5 million in its development.

My visit taught me how central West Virginia University is to the state's bold transformation plan. Much of the vision driving the university comes from president Gordon Gee, whose long career in academia includes five university presidencies in four other states.[63] A charismatic character who's known for his signature bow ties and his social media posts, he's been at the helm of WVU since 2014.

Under Gee's watch, the global management consulting firm McKinsey & Company was charged with identifying high-growth sectors for the state, which has traditionally depended on mining, agriculture, metals manufacturing, and aerospace maintenance. The McKinsey study highlighted potential in cloud services, data centers, and cybersecurity (the FBI already has a national security and intelligence hub in the state). The consultancy also flagged traditional industries such as oil and gas that could be retained and grown, and noted new opportunities arising from shale gas development. The study underscored the need to attract more venture capital, increase the number of STEM graduates, and retain talent. As a result of this research, a consortium led by the universities and the state's department of commerce, called West Virginia Forward, was formed to prioritize innovative ways to fuel the economy.

A related group, Start-up West Virginia, was established to coordinate university-wide efforts to boost the state's innovation economy. While on campus, I interviewed Javier Reyes, then dean of the College of Business and Economics. "West Virginia has tremendous resources and opportunities, but we have to think differently about job creation to move into the future," he told me.[64] "We need to be able to fuel startups and support entrepreneurs with bold ideas that can transform our economy and strengthen the state's economic future."

Such programs could be a much-needed turning point. West Virginia's population has declined over the past decade by 3.2 percent to 1.79 million—the biggest drop nationwide.[65] Lack of job opportunities, poor cell phone and internet penetration, and emigration continue to drain the population, which peaked seventy years ago at 2 million.

The Coal Burnout

My visit to Huntington and Morgantown was full of positives, but the reality of West Virginia's economic condition can't be ignored. The state is actively moving into the digital age, its recent GDP quarterly growth of 7.3 percent is ranked tenth in the nation, and its unemployment rate of 3.6 percent is better than nationwide figures. But its core economic base lags behind. It is the nation's second-largest coal producer after Wyoming, but mining has declined steadily over the last twenty-five years, with an increasing shift toward renewable energy and a rise in use of lower-cost natural gas obtained by fracking.[66]

The state's revival has a lot of work ahead to reverse the negative economic indicators. Consider:

- Despite political claims of "the beauty of West Virginia coal" in campaign rallies, in 2018 the state was producing roughly half its output in 2008, while mining employment had fallen 40 percent to 14,000.[67] This drop-off reflected a similar downward trend nationwide,[68] with Appalachia bearing the brunt of the decline.[69]
- Over the past several decades, offshoring and imports have cost 32,780 West Virginian blue-collar workers their jobs in auto parts, chemical production, aerospace equipment, and metals.[70]

New jobs have been hard to find except for lower-paying retail and service work.

- Manufacturing work made up 13.1 percent of jobs in the state in 1990 but only 6.1 percent by 2017. Mining and logging jobs fell from 5.4 percent of the state's employment to 2.7 percent. Manufacturing shed 35,000 jobs— more than any other sector—while the number of miners declined by 13,000.[71] These figures have tracked steep national declines in manufacturing, mining, and logging jobs.[72]

Socioeconomic indicators are equally bleak. Coal country and hillbilly lands in the five central states of Appalachia have higher poverty and unemployment rates and lower education levels than national and region-wide averages.[73] Appalachia faces a digital divide, with slow or nonexistent high-speed internet and mobile connections.[74] The opioid crisis in rural America continues.[75] West Virginia leads the nation with the highest rates of drug overdose deaths and has the dubious honor of the most smokers of any state.[76]

It's going to be tough to reinvent the wheel in West Virginia. But it's possible to change stereotypical perceptions and to beat hardships. West Virginia showed its ingenuity in leading the nation in distributing COVID vaccine doses. National pharmacy chains wouldn't work as distributors in the rugged mountainous terrain, but family-owned, small-town pharmacies proved up to the task. "The people in the state know how to work together, and they know how to deal with adversity," Brad Smith told me. "I love that we know how to be scrappy. That's the DNA of an entrepreneur."

Fairy Dust?

Can a bit more of Silicon Valley's fairy dust change these Appalachian hills? Remember—the Valley was largely agricultural seven decades ago, until Stanford and Berkeley, engineering talent, startup incubators, and venture capital (plus good weather and beautiful scenery) changed the landscape. The rugged Appalachians have natural beauty; resources; and proud, spirited people. Yes, there is poverty. And the results of a long economic decline. On an earlier trip, when I'd pulled over to ask a local resident for directions, he had attempted to spell the name of the next town, and ended up concluding, "Some people spell it with an E, and others get by just fine without the E." Then, at a roadside restaurant along the east-west Route 68, when I'd ordered a red wine to go with my dinner, the waitress looked perplexed and said, "I had whiine once."

In the poorest rural communities where work is hard to find, the struggles were reflected by the sight of too many run-down trailer parks. There are also places like the centuries-old Greenbrier in White Sulphur Springs, a top-notch resort for business conferences and retreats. Tourism and hospitality—along with healthcare—are bright spots for the state's economy.

The trend toward remote work also creates potential for increased employment in this largely rural state. In summer 2021, Brad and Alys Smith launched Ascend West Virginia, a program created to entice professionals to move to and stay in the Mountain State. Supported by a $25 million gift from the Smiths and the collaboration of the state's tourism agency, the program offers a relocation package of $12,000 in cash and a year's worth of free outdoor recreation rentals for zip-lining, hiking, rafting, and mountain biking. Added to these benefits are free coworking space, professional career development, monthly socials, outdoor recreation, and a welcome trip. The program received 7,500 applications in 2021; 50 candidates were selected initially and 1,000 new residents in all are expected. Preference has been given to outdoor enthusiasts, young families, and those with an entrepreneurial outlook. Groups are moving into three designated places: Morgantown; Lewisburg, in the southern mountains; and the charming village of Shepherdstown, in the Shenandoah Valley along the Potomac River.

"We believe this investment will advance the state's efforts to become the Startup State, a model for the rest of the nation and the world to follow," said Smith. "A silver lining of COVID is that it's given all companies a chance to test how effective and productive their employees can be working from someplace other than the main office."

Smith got the startup wheels spinning in West Virginia with a series of *Shark Tank*–like competitions for Marshall University students. He recruited celebrity judges: actress Jennifer Garner, who was raised in Charleston, and former Marshall and NFL quarterback Chad Pennington. Contestants were tasked with coming up with business concepts using design thinking (an innovation approach used by Intuit) that could improve K-12 literacy in rural areas, introduce students to STEM, and combat a vicious cycle of opiate addiction.

The finalists were flown to Silicon Valley to meet Intuit's founder and were shown around Facebook and Google. Smith has said that the number-one piece of feedback the companies who hosted these visits was: Where do we find more of these individuals? Where did these young men and women come from? "This is why we're continuing to cultivate the 'startup state' mentality that all of us are working on in West Virginia," Smith concluded. He persuaded PayPal CEO Dan Schulman and Adobe Chairman Shantanu Narayen to visit Huntington, where they spoke at the 1928 landmark Keith-Albee Theatre to an audience of 1,800 budding entrepreneurs about the influences that shaped them and the skills and mind-set needed to succeed in today's business world.

Reaching high school students is another prong of this turnaround strategy to groom successive generations and fuel the state's prospects. Smith clued me in to a statewide approach to vocational education and its champion, Kathy D'Antoni. When I met her in Huntington, she described a simulated workplace program where students learn how to run their own business, rotating through CFO, CEO, and marketing roles. With high attendance and graduation rates, the program has been adopted in schools throughout the state. A few of these vocational student projects have received grants from MIT and Sony to implement their creations, such as a wind-tunnel project for the agricultural community and smart-home technology for the elderly. An associate school superintendent turned education consultant, D'Antoni said this project-based trade learning could become a model nationwide and pointed out that school system educators from twenty-five states have observed it.

Online, I met with one of the program's budding stars, Payton Brown, a high-school student doing simulated workplace training at the Nicholas County Career and Technical Center. He had invented a collapsible, portable chicken coop, equipped with a mobile app that beeps to signal a laid egg. He wore a wide-brimmed cowboy hat, called me *ma'am*, and responded to my questions directly without a trace of shyness. He lives at his family's 200-acre farm with no internet, but he connected from his grandparents' house.

Brown told me he's selling his e-chicken coop in nearby counties and wants to broaden sales to urban areas. "These are two-foot coops, so they're small enough for a terrace or balcony," he pointed out. The coops are designed in an A-frame with hinges at the top and come with a web-camera setup—and two chickens with leg bracelets for monitoring. Asked why two hens, he responded, "Chickens like to have friends." His dad is helping him saw logs on the family farm to build the coops, which he looks to sell for $500 to $1200. He's in a trial phase. "Right now, we're cutting out all the kinks, seeing how well the post office can handle it, and how well the chickens will do if they are shipped cross-country. I plan to go full-scale next year after I graduate," he said. I was impressed with his confidence. Brown is learning more carpentry skills at the entrepreneurial center and recently received a governor's workforce award for maintaining a high grade-point average, keeping a good attendance record, and testing drug-free.

Smith is encouraged by such young people reaching for the stars yet knows the limitations. "What we have to overcome is a mind-set that 'No one's ever going to fund me, even if I come up with a great idea.' We have to be willing to actually get out there and show people that we know how to build things, and then, once success happens, other success will happen. So it's about having a growth mind-set and not a fixed mind-set. By the way, this is not a pejorative statement. It is the reality in most places I visit, other than in [Silicon] Valley and a couple other places where people believe everything is possible. We just have to overcome that. I like to say 'Lean into the win.' That's what we have to do. The heartland has to do that; it has to believe in itself."

Long Road Ahead

I left West Virginia feeling positive about the state's chances, with icons like Smith, Chambers, and Lane providing so much support and young people like Kelly Leonard and Payton Brown taking advantage of new opportunities. Confidence, courage, and action are required and are more and more possible with the leadership, determination, and capital the tech icons are importing. They're helping to create a new zeitgeist where college graduates don't have to go out of state for work.

Yet the region is still early in its development. There's a long road ahead. It takes leadership to spur change, get out of a downward cycle, and improve morale. But will it be enough? Skeptics wonder if West Virginia will retain the best minds in the world as Stanford can. Will a tech genius from India want to move to or work in West Virginia? Some might, but you need thousands. If that is to happen, the heartland will need more than outside help—it will need town champions who are restoring their home places with all the energy and muscle they've got.

Chapter Six

Town Champions

How pioneering city leaders in Portsmouth, Ohio—lawyer, professor, real estate developer, and legendary tycoon—are mobilizing a cleanup with a lasting impact

At the former Calvary Baptist Church in Portsmouth, Ohio, Jeremy Burnside enthusiastically showed me around his law office. He had purchased this old church building when the congregation outgrew the space, and he repurposed it for his practice, leaving the pews and a pulpit in place to use as part of a mock courtroom. Burnside may be the only attorney in the country who can prepare his clients for their cases in a trial, from a lectern. He goes through testimony from a fake witness stand and practices cross-examination before a judge and a courtroom full of spectators.

Preparing for this leg of my trip, I came across a press release from a community group called Friends of Portsmouth that included a quote from Burnside about how the city is "resigning its position as the national opioid crisis punching bag and is swapping its battered image for fresh paint and Guinness world records." That sounded intriguing, so I connected with Burnside on LinkedIn, phoned him, and we arranged to meet.

At the confluence of the Ohio and Scioto Rivers, Portsmouth is in south Ohio, on the Kentucky border. It was once an industrious river town making iron, steel, and shoes. It lies eighty miles south of my hometown of Lancaster, traveling on country routes, then a straight run down US 23. On my way there, as I passed the pyramid-shaped hills in the distance and the CSX coal trains going north to Lake Erie, I saw a billboard with a giant photo of Burnside, his office phone number 740-354-HURT, and the address of his personal injury practice. When I got to his office, I met an affable, smart-talking, high-energy attorney who let me know of his distinguished ancestor, Ambrose Burnside, the Civil War general so famous for his prominent side whiskers that they became known as *sideburns*—a play on his last name.

The Burnside I met was the founder and chief cheerleader of Friends of Portsmouth, which is a nonprofit community development organization seeking to rebuild this small town on the Ohio River and alter its image as the opioid capital of the nation. He organizes pep rallies, parades, and clean-up days and tirelessly boasts how the city is on the road to recovery.

"We are leading the nation in recovery and resurgence. I challenge anyone to show me a town of this size that has accomplished what we have in two years," Burnside proclaimed. We were seated at a conference room table upstairs, while he thumbed through a stack of newspaper clippings about Portsmouth's downturn and potential for a comeback. It was obvious he was eager to spread the good word about his hometown. He had urged national media to document the town's revitalization, and though several *New York Times* reporters had detailed the city's struggles, few had covered any upside. While the pill mills that illegally prescribed opioids had been shut down, the devastation ran deep.

"The image of our downtown needed to change immediately so we could start believing in ourselves again. Our downtown felt like it looked. Weeds, corrosion, and desolation," Burnside said. "The city looked like the despair that the national media had been reporting about us." (Shortly after my visit, Burnside was diagnosed with brain cancer and passed away in mid-2022. The town is still processing his loss.)

Down-home Roots

Born and raised in Cleveland, Burnside never forgot his down-home roots. Like many from Appalachia, his paternal grandparents had moved north after the coal mines closed and the factories shut. He attended the University of Charleston in West Virginia, where he was president of the student body, editor of the yearbook, and captain of the rowing team. After graduation he pursued a law degree at the Appalachian School of Law in Grundy, Virginia, and he would chronicle his roller-coaster experience as a law student in a self-published book. During five years litigating in northern Ohio, he missed the folksiness of Appalachian culture and settled in Portsmouth in 2009.

The town faced intense challenges. In 1940, 40,000 lived there; now only half that number call it home. One-third live in poverty and 17 percent of the town's high school students are dropouts.[77,78] It was a familiar heartland tale: another burned-out Rust Belt city with faded factories that no longer made shoes or steel. In the 1950s, the town's major mill employed 4,800. By 1980, it shut down its furnaces, costing 1,124 jobs. A coke plant operated with about 200 workers until it was closed in 2002 and the structure razed in 2007. Now a Walmart operates on the once-contaminated land.[79]

But the efforts of Burnside and others at community cleanup were encouraging—a microcosm of a region-wide rebuild of Greater Appalachia, which is beginning to renew economic vitality. I had seen this rebuild gathering steam in other parts of the state. The Cleveland-based real estate tycoon and philanthropist Albert Ratner, now in his nineties, had been supporting and guiding impoverished Ohio counties as they up-skilled their workforce. Such high-profile champions and the townspeople they inspire were creating positive energy and mobilizing local government, universities, medical centers, businesses, and economic development organizations.

This rebuild was not about becoming bed-and-breakfast tourist destinations. Civic leaders were tackling chronic issues: talent fleeing, lack of opportunities, poverty, and drug addiction. Without such efforts, poverty-stricken, population-losing places of the deindustrialized Rust Belt could have been left in socioeconomic ruins. But Ratner, Burnside, and many others were determined not to let that happen.

In prep for my Portsmouth visit, Burnside sent links demonstrating the community's engagement in revitalizing this injured Ohio town. A small army of volunteers had organized trash pickups every month, chili cook-off fund-raisers, block parties, rock concerts, and publicity-seeking challenges like the setting of Guinness world records. Have you heard about the record number of people potting plants simultaneously (1,485)? Or the most people caroling at one time (1,880)? Portsmouth set both these world records.

Or how about the city's pep rally? Burnside invited media to attend a press conference for what he labeled a "parade of positivity." From an impromptu stage near the bank of the Ohio River, he launched an imaginative PR campaign for the city, while cheerleaders waved pom-poms and rock music blared. Town ambassadors from the university, businesses, cultural and counseling centers, and government spoke. They celebrated the return of the national powerboat championships to Portsmouth for the first time in thirty years, a race my uncle Homer entered long ago.

More than twenty-eight downtown property renovations and improvements costing $12 million were highlighted during that rally, including a new dog-walking park and a $2.4 million riverfront project with upgraded boat launches and docks. "This was our response to decades of negativity, a way of showing our community, the press, and the nation what we are really all about—positive energy and community involvement," Burnside said.

Burnside brought me downtown, where he showed me around the historic Boneyfiddle commercial neighborhood, which maintains a look of the 1860s with twenty properties on the National Registry of Historic Places. On Second Street, he pointed out a new health food store, a pottery studio, a bar and grill, several antique stores, and a new hotel. This was the same street my cousin Judy warned me to avoid; it was a "real bad place" when she was growing up next door to my grandparents' farmhouse, about twelve miles north of Portsmouth. We also visited the Kricker Innovation Hub, an 1890s building that once housed a clothing manufacturer and was refashioned by Shawnee State University into a flexible work space that can also hold entrepreneurship programs. Burnside proudly showed me the three downtown buildings he and his wife, real estate broker Maddie Burnside, purchased and are restoring. Two of their side-by-side structures on Second Street have historical value as a front for the Underground

Railroad. A bad windstorm had just knocked out a façade, but Burnside was still hoping to turn one into a video game arcade and another as a headquarters space for Friends of Portsmouth.

There were plenty more projects on the to-do list, including restoration of the weathered football stadium where the NFL's Portsmouth Spartans played from 1928 until 1934, when the franchise was sold and became the Detroit Lions. A massive plan entitled Elevate Portsmouth calls for turning this stadium into a public venue, though the dream of bringing back a professional sports team seems unlikely to materialize.

Yet cleanup projects won't work in isolation. Robert Horton, director of Scioto County Economic Development, put it to me this way: "The people in the private sector in Boneyfiddle who are cleaning up downtown and rehabilitating old buildings won't be enough if the rest of the town doesn't come along." But Burnside was staying optimistic and proactive. On our downtown tour, he showed me the Glockner Museum, a three-story, red-brick, recently refurbished building that is home to the Glockner family's collection of memorabilia from six generations in horse trading, bicycle sales, and auto dealerships—and also a speakeasy bar hidden down a flight of stairs accessed from an opening behind a fake bookcase. It's the same Glockner family that wrote a $2 million check to launch PureCycle Technologies' facility, the innovative recycling company I had visited in Ironton.

We went into the bustling Market Street Café, where I ordered a sandwich and began reminiscing. I had some family history here. I told Burnside about the True Value hardware stores my grandfather owned, one in town that was family-run for over forty years. (Family legend has it that my grandfather made a fortune when TVs first came out, offering free antennas on a trial basis and getting customers hooked on television.) A funny thing: I tracked down the fellow who had taken over the store from my relatives, and he remembered my grandfather dropping promotional flyers from the sky as he flew his private airplane over town. Quite the entrepreneur!

Portsmouth Networking

Burnside invited a couple of pals in the Portsmouth cleanup to our meeting: Sean Dunne, a city councilman, and local entrepreneur and real estate developer Tim Wolfe. A transplant from Ireland, where he earned a PhD from Trinity College Dublin, Dunne teaches sociology at Shawnee State University, a former technical and community college that started in 1945 as a branch of OU. It's named after the fierce warrior Shawnee Indians who, led by their chief Tecumseh, settled in the lower Scioto River valley. The small college excels in practical studies that can lead to marketable job skills, such as plastics engineering technology and video game design, one of the nation's top-ranked programs in the nation.

Dunne was drawn to Portsmouth and his teaching post by the opportunity to make a difference by applying social sciences to the city's recovery. At Shawnee, he introduced a minor in grant-writing. He engaged his students in applications for community improvement grants such as restoring the municipal stadium and constructing a skate park. Portsmouth, he said, was "trying to get away from a pure manufacturing base. We're not sitting around waiting for a big factory to come back but are creating a university that can help to revive the community."

The executive director of Friends of Portsmouth, Wolfe is a military veteran and engineer who rebuilt high schools and hospitals in Iraq after the US invasion in 2003. A few years later he returned to his native Portsmouth, where he found former high school friends in the throes of addiction. He set up his own business, Eflow Development Group, to work on construction and remodeling of downtown buildings, and opened the Patties & Pints bar and grill, with remodeled apartments upstairs. The restaurant became a hangout for the group restoring Portsmouth. Wolfe also serves on the board of the local counseling center, and he has been training recovering addicts in construction and restoration. He said his goal was to "build a local labor force to handle a construction boom."

The town's best-known entrepreneurial hero is Dale King. After multiple deployments to Iraq as an army intelligence officer, King returned home and opened a CrossFit studio. With his partner, Renee Wallace, he also started Doc Spartan, a company that sells a popular skincare ointment. They nailed $75,000 as an investment during an episode of the TV show *Shark Tank*, sealed with his pitch about a veteran returning to a broken-down town and reviving it with new business. Today he employs Portsmouth residents, several of them recovering addicts. King also has partnered with the counseling center to launch an experimental program incorporating fitness training into addiction-treatment programs.

Worn-out Shoes

A good example of the evolution of Portsmouth's economic history (and the history of many heartland cities and towns) is its footwear industry. In the 1930s, more than two thousand Portsmouth residents were employed at the Selby Shoe Company and nearly as many at the Excelsior Shoe Factory. In the 1950s, 16 percent of the city's workforce labored at these factories. I remember seeing Selby's blocks-long red-brick complex and hearing that my grandmother worked there as a teen. Closed in 1957, the factory was demolished in the late 1990s.

Over the decades, the shoe industry was virtually wiped out as manufacturing moved to Central America and Asia. By the mid-1970s, all that remained was a shoelace maker, Mitchellace Shoe String Company,[80] which survived into the 2000s. It was about to close in 2009 due to foreign competition when a group of local businesspeople put up their own money to rescue it. They changed the name to Sole Choice and refocused the business on 100 percent made-in-the-USA shoelaces. During the pandemic, Sole Choice expanded its product line of shoelaces and accessories to cords for COVID-fighting masks. Now, in a sign of the times, the business has downsized to a small building nearby. Its former factory is being redeveloped into a centralized counseling center to treat up to 260 patients in two-to-three-month treatment programs.

Bill Dingus, executive director of the Lawrence Economic Development Corporation and the Greater Lawrence County Chamber of Commerce, has described the change this way: "Unfortunately, the growth industry is the drug rehabilitation industry. When Walmart is your largest employer, it is a sad day." The region's coal industry was seeing an upturn until about eight years ago, when natural gas prices fell 50 percent and "knocked the bottom out of the coal industry," Dingus told me. Many of the area's several coal-fired power plants have closed, making ghost towns of the little communities built around those facilities.

Outside of the universities and hospitals, the region's main employer is the data center and communications equipment provider Vertiv, which has about six hundred employees. And there are four small industrial companies. "The main note of this is that the private sector firms are no longer the lead employers of the area. Today, the public, not-for-profits, and large retailers are the employment leaders with minimal to moderate wage structures," Dingus said. "There are no new shopping complexes, and the Dollar Stores are taking the region by storm."

The much-touted opportunity zones that provide tax incentives for investors in economically distressed communities are starting to have some impact.[81] Such zones in southeastern Ohio led to the development of a new hotel in downtown Portsmouth and redevelopment of the Greater Portsmouth Regional Airport—where my grandfather kept his Cessna and sometimes gave rides to us kids. I found it amazing to drive a new shortcut from the airport, a superhighway stretching sixteen miles that provided hilltop views of farmland below, before bypassing the city of Portsmouth and intersecting Route 52 along the Ohio River. This Appalachian engineering marvel costing $634 million and taking nearly a decade to complete seems out of place with the winding country roads close by my grandparents' acres on Gampp Lane and the little Scioto River. But it does open a direct commercial route and cuts travel time between the airport and river by twenty minutes.

President Biden's $1 trillion infrastructure plan, with $110 billion to improve the nation's roads, bridges, ports, and water systems and another $65 billion to expand high-speed internet, could also give the Appalachian Ohio region a boost. It calls for investing $21 billion to put thousands to work in cleaning up now idled and polluted industrial and energy sites, and putting $65 billion into renewable-energy and cleantech projects, with a priority on funds for rural areas.

Ohio's local communities also stand to benefit from $808 million to settle opioid-related lawsuits—part of a broader $26 billion deal in 2022 between state and local governments and several drug manufacturers and distributors for their role in the opioid epidemic, which led to 500,000 overdose deaths nationally from 1999 to 2019,[82] including 39,000 deaths in Ohio. Scioto County was the lone hold-out in the Ohio settlement, its officials deciding that the $1.8 million share it stood to receive was insufficient given that no other area had been hit harder.

Pivotal Juncture

The opioid crisis in this part of the world—the world where I grew up—is at a pivotal juncture. The pain clinics that illegally prescribed what was known as hillbilly heroin were shut over a decade ago. As many as twenty doctors were imprisoned. Trafficking of fentanyl was curtailed and more than a dozen rehab centers were opened to help addicts recover. But the problems persist, and the drug overdose cycle hasn't been broken in Portsmouth's Scioto County[83]: it was aggravated during the coronavirus outbreak by limited social interaction and high unemployment. The crime rate remains high, and those with drug problems have moved to back alleys or the internet.[84]

The two worlds of Portsmouth—and the heartland—continue to exist side by side. On a return visit, I saw the city's Hallmark-like Christmas displays and took time to see Portsmouth's flood wall and its colorful murals depicting the Ohio River Valley's Indian mound builders burial suites and 2,000 years of local history—a marker of the city's recovery after the devastating Ohio River flood of 1937. But I felt concerned enough about the possibility of drug-related crime to keep my car locked. On the other hand, the efforts of Jeremy Burnside, Sean Dunne, Tim Wolfe, and others provided me with tremendous encouragement, convincing me that the will, expertise, and passion are there to make the turnaround that I had been seeing throughout the heartland a reality at the local level.

Project GRIT

As I left Scioto County to cross the Ohio River and trek deeper into rural Appalachia, I drove by the county's career center. I had been alerted to this center by an unlikely source—Albert Ratner, the Cleveland business mogul who helped to develop landmark projects across the country, including the Navy Yard in Brooklyn, the Charleston Town Center, and Tower City in Cleveland. Despite his advanced age, he has been actively advising several community leaders on boosting economic growth, improving education, and providing jobs for youth in Appalachia.

I had spoken to Ratner on a Zoom call. He told me that he got involved in working to reduce poverty and increase opportunities for Ohioans after a government jobs plan didn't seem to be working. He formed Future Plans, a training and coaching company, with career adviser Denise Reading. Future Plans "hasn't made any profits yet," he told me, but that wasn't its purpose. "The idea is that you can change poverty or the income differential and improve life spans and medical care. We can help to create a real opportunity if people want the opportunity, and help them determine where they want to be."

In thinking about how to help Appalachian Ohio, Ratner asked himself what the region had that others didn't. It had high unemployment and drug addiction problems, but it also had rehab centers and a population that could be trained. Plus a low cost of living and plenty of vacant land. And since COVID, a lot of work has become virtual or remote.

Ratner's idea was to create "Zoom towns" throughout Appalachia, where remote, trained workforces could live in lower-cost regions and earn money at virtual centers for employers. "There's a real opportunity in Appalachia if people want it," Ratner said. "Everybody should have the opportunity to do the best they can. Many people don't believe it can be done. But if you take care of the people around you, there is a better opportunity for the Rust Belt to grow."

Ratner has also been involved with Project GRIT (Growing Rural Independence Together through Jobs), a pilot program for five southeastern Ohio counties with state funding and local resources that is intended to develop a skilled workforce and placement in well-matched jobs. A good example of GRIT's effort has been a program set up with the South Central Ohio Educational Service Center and the Scioto County Career Technical Center. Their initial goal is to hire 300 trained workers after applications are screened and interviews completed.

Ratner has also counseled Cara Dingus Brook, president and CEO of the Foundation for Appalachian Ohio, which raised $150 million in philanthropic funds for grants, scholarships, and wi-fi hot spots for towns without internet access. When I spoke with Brook about Ratner's mentorship, she said, "Into his nineties, he's working with us on turning Appalachia around and bringing back jobs. We are addressing long-term problems. It is not so much about the money but about the mind-set—a culture of diminished expectations."

My tour through the Appalachian hills was certainly marked by signs of decline, and I couldn't help wincing at all-too-frequent improper grammar: "I *ain't gonna* do it." And "We *was* there." There's not a lot of hustle. But people are kind-hearted and generous and eager to help you out. There's a special quality in the heartland that never leaves you, no matter how far you roam. This sense of belonging and community can be harnessed to improve lifestyles and work and to rebuild cities and towns like Portsmouth. It's time, as President Biden has emphasized, to grow the economy "from the bottom up and the middle out," rewarding labor, not just wealth along the coasts, and creating a culture of brighter expectations for more folks.

If the grassroots efforts such as those I discovered in southeastern Ohio work, community-led redevelopment could serve as a model for rebuilding the Appalachian foothills from the ground up. The result could be a wider and deeper entrepreneurial river, the triumph of progress over stagnation, lightness over dark adversity.

Part Four

Locales and Resources

Chapter Seven

The Innovation Districts

*How heartland cities and towns are creating local resources
to help businesses regain competitiveness*

Innovation districts are a critically important component of the heartland's turnaround. Supported by government and corporate funding, these hubs have sprung up throughout former rusted-out regions. Each tends to specialize in a particular technology, individually leveraging their traditions and strengths. Many have already created breakthrough startups on a national level in such important fields as healthcare, security, transportation, and finance.

So far, this book has described how, during the height of the pandemic, I traveled the heartland in search of individual innovators, corporate allies, and venture capitalists who are, together, transforming the Midwest. In this chapter I want to relate how, on that same journey, I discovered the way in which cities and towns are supporting these players by creating innovation districts that are not just enabling new businesses but transforming communities. I started by going in search of a good example in my family's home state. Who would expect to find a new-age tech business in Appalachian Ohio? Yet, in rural Columbiana County, in the town of Leetonia, twenty-five miles south of Youngstown, I came across a sixty-three-year-old, family-owned business, Humtown Products, that has pivoted its old-line foundry to using state-of-the-art 3D printing technologies.

Mark Lamoncha is Humtown's owner and president. When I drove to Columbiana to meet him, I had trouble finding the nondescript alleyway that leads to his plant. I pulled over and called Mark. He could see my car a half mile down the road, told me to sit tight, then drove out to meet me and guide me in. I saw that as a heartland experience—folks being hospitable and practical no matter what the occasion.

Mark's dad founded the business in 1959, and Mark had worked hard since then to keep the family enterprise in tune with the times. But the market crash of 2008 hit the company hard, and the 220-employee business lost the majority of its team and almost went bankrupt. Desperate, Lamoncha tried buying lottery tickets. He prayed. By means of vision, innovation, and hard work, he kept Humtown going from year to year until he hit a breakthrough in 2014, when the company adopted a new-fangled, 3D printing production technique for his conventional foundry business—part of the backbone of the machine-tool industry that has been slowing dying out in America.[85]

Additive manufacturing—printing objects layer by layer from computerized designs—is the innovative process that allowed Lamoncha to keep his remaining forty-eight employees. He boosted productivity by basing pay rates on output, measured in a game-like competition, thereby shortening turnaround times and reducing the scrap rate. The firm could also customize products on demand.

This additive division of the business would eventually account for 55 percent of the company's revenues and helped Humtown retain corporate customers such as Caterpillar, GE, and Cummins. The turnaround led to Humtown Products winning the 2020 National Association of Manufacturer's top award for leadership and technological innovation. The business got further notice when its full-size, 3D-printed bobblehead of Donald Trump stood watch in Cleveland during the 2016 Republican convention.

Lamoncha could not have accomplished this on his own. He relied on a cluster of local, specialized resources—a growing trend in the heartland as businesses of all sorts strive to stay afloat by adapting to advanced technology. Meeting him, I understood how, in a region dealing with all kinds of problems, Appalachian resourcefulness is a key part of the heartland's rebirth. This resourcefulness is both individual—tough-minded women and men doing what they need to do—and social—communities coming together to support each other in hard times. This combination of traits is the foundation of a brighter future for towns that once boomed with auto- and steel-making success and now must change or die. "We have a culture of making things," congressman Tim Ryan has said. And manufacturing innovators like Humtown are fueling the transition from Steel Belt to Tech Belt.

I walked Humtown's shop-room floor with Lamoncha, who has led this three-generation family business since 1995. We passed piles of sandbags and half a dozen 3D printing machines whirring away. He spoke of the importance of innovation. "This was our Kodak moment," he said. "If you are not in the next space, you are out of business. Look no further than Kodak and Blockbuster. In hundreds of years, nothing has been this big a paradigm shift. Humtown has been around since 1959. Casting has been around since the Egyptians, and not a lot has changed in the metal casting industry. But this kind of change? This is amazing!"

Capable of making intricate products without costly tooling, additive production techniques have evolved quickly to a $10-billion-plus industry globally in the wider $12 trillion manufacturing sector.[86] Its quick adoption in the aerospace, automotive, and medical equipment markets is driving 14.4 percent industry growth, and a projected $23.8 billion global market by 2027.[87] Humtown is a small company that has plugged into a growing trend, not just in terms of the new technology it uses but in its willingness to combine individual initiative with a broad, community-based effort to change the region's manufacturing landscape. Mark was able to leverage local resources in a hub of advanced manufacturing resources in northeast Ohio. Government-supported economic boosters such as the Youngstown Business Incubator and America Makes introduced him to the new technology. He also was able to recruit technical talent and secure 3D printing machines from Youngstown State University and its Center for Innovation in Advanced Manufacturing. Now, this modernized portion of

Humtown's overall business is increasing by more than 50 percent annually, and eight additional employees have been hired. "We were between the 'get set' and 'go,' and now we're into the 'go' phase of growth," Lamoncha said about the turnaround.

The Building Blocks of Innovation

Throughout the heartland, tech-centric innovation hubs are the building blocks for a region-wide rebuild, replacing abandoned factories and mines. From Pittsburgh to Youngstown to Indianapolis, midwestern cities are vying to become mini–Silicon Valleys. Each magnet city builds on its own core strengths and technological specialties. All are going for higher-skilled, better-paying innovative jobs, economic growth, livable workplace zones, and community vigor.

These switched-on, midsized midwestern boomtowns aggregate localized talent, startups, universities, research institutes, corporations, science parks, accelerators, incubators, and coworking facilities—often in renovated red-brick industrial buildings. Civic amenities like museums, good transit, and vibrant downtowns add to the mix. The tech build-out is bringing in high-skilled engineers, software developers, research scientists, data analysts, and product managers. All these young businesses need accounting, legal, and banking services. This creates a cluster effect, a synergy of like-minded, motivated people.

The large midwestern cities have the scale to collect this talent and create hubs of innovation. I saw it on my travels: Detroit, Pittsburgh, Columbus, Cincinnati, Cleveland, and Indianapolis all impressed me, and the data prove it: they score high for market depth, vitality, and appeal if not quite the high-energy, creative concentrated environment of, say, Cambridge or Palo Alto.[88] College towns stand out too, such as Ann Arbor, with the University of Michigan in the heart of the city. Although many Rust Belt cities are still losing population, several have seen socioeconomic gains over the past decade, such as a higher percentage of college graduates and lower poverty rates (see table C).

I met plenty of entrepreneurs thriving from this growth, including Matt Buder Shapiro, cofounder of the AI-driven healthcare billing platform MedPilot. In 2018, he relocated his young business from New York to Cleveland, and he hasn't looked back. His startup was seeded with $3.5 million, led by Northeast Ohio's Valley Growth Ventures, and was bought in early 2021 by the New Jersey–based health-tech provider Vytalize, which raised $50 million in venture capital a year later. Shapiro is a Cleveland native. "There's already more than enough attention to the coasts as hubs of strong talent and opportunity," he told me. "In the Greater Cleveland area, we have been blown away by the level of healthcare expertise, drive, and grit that our employee base has shown. With no difficulty, we have tapped people with specialized skills in sales, finance, customer service, and technology."

Yet the San Francisco Bay area continues to be the gold standard for tech talent. No place comes close to its social and economic openness to disruptive ideas, diverse population, abundant venture capital, and technological know-how. California leads the nation by far in recent US patent grants.[89] "Silicon Valley will always have a leadership role in tech talent because of its risk-taking culture and tolerance of failure," Ro Khanna, who represents Silicon Valley in Congress, explained to me. However, he acknowledged what seems inevitable: "This lead may be more distributed in the future."

Ohio wants a piece of this redistribution and is allocating billions to develop urban innovation districts in Cincinnati, Cleveland, and Columbus. The goal? To create thousands of jobs in high tech, healthcare, and smart manufacturing and to educate students in STEM fields, anchored by local academic institutions, research outfits, medical facilities, and corporations.

But it's not only Ohio. There are cities showing unexpected success, such as Louisville, which is seeing a strong increase in tech employment and where corporate anchors like Humana and United Parcel Service have provided a springboard for healthcare and logistics innovations to emerge and the startup organizations Amplify and Endeavor have offered a road map for entrepreneurs. With their organizational support, I gathered a roundtable of Louisville business leaders to discuss the city's future. "We can't play every bet on the board, or we will lose every bet on the board," Tony Ellis, executive director of Kentucky Innovation, said during that meeting. He pointed out that logistics and healthcare were "easy spots" for the city and provided diversity from longtime employers such as Ford, GE Appliances, and Brown-Forman.

As Silicon Valley decentralizes and new hot spots emerge, innovation districts mash together startups, coworking spaces, venture hubs, lively bars, universities, cafes, retail, and housing. Short North in Columbus—north of downtown and short of Ohio State University—is a great example. Steep real estate prices on the coasts have led millennial home buyers, who comprise 36 percent of purchases, to move inland. A ranking of the top twenty cities for this age group shows several midwestern cities scoring high for affordability, livability, and job opportunities.[90]

Fueling the Comeback

My midpandemic journey through the heartland took in many of these hot spots and showed me how grassroots innovation is working by relying on a mobilization of resources within a tech community. In Youngstown, Ohio, I saw the bustle of its steel past starting to return. Youngstown Business Incubator (YBI) is a brick in that rebuilding, amplifying this region's heritage of making things. YBI is a five-building tech manufacturing campus, which includes the national accelerator America Makes, a $70 million collaborative innovation center, and an additive manufacturing facility, all of which leverage the expertise and facilities of nearby Youngstown State University. YBI's CEO is Barb Ewing, former economic development director for Tim Ryan.

The Youngstown incubator opened in 1995 on the city's main drag, where Reichart Furniture's showroom and warehouse once flourished. With government funding to accelerate new technologies, Ewing and previous CEO Jim Cossler laid the groundwork over two decades for this full-fledged incubator, which also wraps in the microventure fund Valley Growth Ventures as a startup investor.

My tour of the campus began at Tech Block Building 5, a 65,000-square-foot space renovated in late 2017 and loaded with 3D printing machines. It also houses ten startups—with more coming in a build-out. The printing presses of Youngstown's local newspaper, *The Vindicator*, used to be here. Salvaged in the remake was a single hot-metal typesetting machine, which is on display near the entrance. From there I visited the headquarters of America

Makes, a flagship institute formed in 2012 by the Obama administration to secure leadership in 3D technology and speed up its adoption. The showroom is full of 3D-printed industrial parts. I just missed former secretary of commerce Wilbur Ross on location in July 2020 to present a $1.4 million grant here for production of 3D-printed personal protective equipment.

Cossler described the journey. "It's been hard for Youngstown. We didn't have indigenous tech companies. We didn't have a Cleveland Clinic. We didn't have sufficient university spin-outs. Given the lack of resources, we couldn't be good at everything. We didn't want to be mediocre at all things but to be world class in a domain." One of Cossler's missions as CEO was convincing fellow Youngstowners to ditch a sense of inferiority and to believe in themselves.

Within a decade of its start, the incubator's stable of companies grew to employ 540 workers and generate $17.8 million in revenues. Educational-tools manufacturer Turning Technologies became a midsized company with its own headquarters in the government-funded Taft Technology Center, the first new building downtown in seventy-five years.

"Fifteen years ago, we asked ourselves a critical question about the corridor stretching from Pittsburgh to Cleveland. What happened to the best and brightest when they couldn't find high-paying jobs?" Cossler said. He combed LinkedIn, looking for successful executives who had moved away but whose connections could be helpful. They delivered. Eric Spiegel, former CEO of Siemens USA, donated $440 million in software and training to Youngstown State University. George Pavlov, CEO of Bayshore Global, the family office managing Google cofounder Sergey Brin's wealth, set up a scholarship for local students of color and steered portfolio companies to work with the incubator.

Youngstown's success also has an international dimension. Barak Rabinowitz, managing partner at the Israeli fund F2 Venture Capital and operator of an additive manufacturing accelerator, grew up watching Youngstown's young people going elsewhere for jobs as its factories and steel mills closed their doors. He met Ewing on a delegation to Israel in 2017. That meeting led to a collaboration, enabling Israeli

3D startups such as PrintSyst to gain an American launching pad and the YBI incubator to secure an Israeli XJet, an advanced 3D machine for printing on ceramics and metals.

Federal funding helped propel this new technology with the establishment of the Youngstown State University's Center for Innovation in Additive Manufacturing. Graduates can be fairly confident of a well-paying job of $70,000 or more at General Electric, General Motors, and Caterpillar. Or they could find work locally at large steel-tube manufacturer Vallourec, which recently invested $650 million in a new plant alongside its current mill to produce upgraded seamless pipe used in the oil and gas industry—Youngstown's biggest capital project in a half-century.

The Youngstown hub effect also enables entrepreneurs to start their own businesses by harnessing the advanced manufacturing resources in the city. I saw two startups in action at Tech Block Building 5. JuggerBot3d designs and builds industrial-grade additive manufacturing machines costing upward of $25,000. Goodyear is a customer. When I stopped by, cofounders and recent graduates Zachary DiVencenzo and Dan Fernback were tinkering with their human-sized industrial 3D printer capable of making sections nearly the size of a Smart Car. Their business is bulking up after securing $100,000 from the state-backed Innovation Fund Northeast Ohio and aligning with Brilex Group, a local heavy-machining manufacturer, and the Oak Ridge National Laboratory, which, believe it or not, created the world's first 3D-printed car.

Downstairs, I saw Fitz Frames making 3D-printed eyeglass frames. A custom design is made from a mobile-app photo of the customer's face and molded in three snap-in parts, with the wearer's signature printed inside. CEO Gabriel Schlumberger hatched the business idea after constantly replacing his kids' broken glasses. In this era of decentralized working, Schlumberger lives in Los Angeles and outsources production to his Youngstown team, making for a product fully designed and manufactured in the US. At the outset of the virus, Fitz Frames added production of protective eyewear for frontline healthcare professionals, made and delivered within ten days—with a waitlist of 4,000. Innovation is all about adaptability!

During my stay in downtown Youngstown, I saw people taking a lunch break and smoking cigarettes on the sidewalk, while kids Rollerbladed past. I visited the historic movie palace where the Warner brothers got their start in vaudeville. The city felt both historic and contemporary, and it was difficult to reconcile the high tech environment I was seeing with the city's reputation for corruption and danger. During a phone interview, Youngstown's mayor, Jamael Tito Brown, was candid about the past. "Historically, Youngstown was always a place to know someone, to get it done, or to pay someone to get it done." But today, he said, "we are open for business and eager to bring Youngstown forward together. One of the pieces of our

Tech Hubs and Innovation Specialties

- **Youngstown:** 3D printing to make products from industrial to consumer with resources from government-supported incubators and talent from Youngstown State University
- **Detroit**: Advanced manufacturing for the factory floor tied to automotive companies undergoing major transition, entry of EV startups, and real estate redevelopment
- **Dayton:** Cybersecurity, defense spawned by proximity to Wright-Patterson Air Force Base resources and push by opportunity zones
- **Cincinnati:** Packaged goods evolving from base for Procter & Gamble leadership and culture, numerous tech startup advocates including Kroger, and startup accelerators
- **Columbus:** Insurtech and healthtech startups fed by corporates such as Nationwide Insurance, R&D base from Ohio State University, and Battelle; sufficient venture funding from Drive Capital and governmental services for entrepreneurs; data centers set up by Google, Amazon, Facebook
- **Indianapolis:** Software-as-a-Service (SaaS) management tools originating from Salesforce acquisition of local startup ExactTarget and resulting formation of High Alpha Venture Studio
- **Cleveland:** Biotech advancements stemming from healthtech cluster with entrepreneurial bioscientists at Cleveland Clinic and Case Western Reserve University
- **Pittsburgh:** Robotics and AI grown out of Carnegie Mellon University's engineering and computer science focus, as well as launch of well-funded, self-driving unicorn companies including Aurora

progress is a move from steel to additive manufacturing." He added that the downtown's real estate market is picking up, which I'd noticed from residents coming and going from apartment buildings. "We are seeing a low vacancy rate downtown, and properties are not staying on the market long." Spacious studios at a well-renovated downtown tower rent for $1,000 monthly—a bargain compared with Silicon Valley or Manhattan.

Detroit is another midwestern city undergoing renewal. Most people see it as a yesteryear city that endured the 1967 riots, muddled through the auto industry collapse, and declared bankruptcy in 2013. Or perhaps they reflect on the Motown Sound soulful music of the 1960s that began when many African Americans moved from the South to Detroit to work in the auto factories. Today, the former auto-making capital of the world, which has three remaining assembly plants downtown, is reinventing its Motor City reputation with electric vehicles and self-driving technology. Ford is investing $740 million to renovate the Michigan Central Train Station and its associated tower into a research hub for tests of self-driving cars. In 2018 Ford bought the depot, which had been vacant and deteriorating since the last Amtrak rolled out thirty years earlier. Plans for a new central Detroit rail station that loops in buses, bikes, and ride-hailing services would be a welcome improvement. General Motors has earmarked $2.2 billion to transform its Detroit-Hamtramck plant as Factory Zero, its first EV assembly operation. And EV maker Rivian, backed by Ford and Amazon, has tested electric vans in the city, too.

To remake its industrial base, Detroit has zeroed in on manufacturing innovation known as Industry 4.0, or advanced and automated production techniques, which brings digitization to the factory floor using data analytics, robotics, augmented reality, and the Internet of Things (IoT). Invisible AI, a computer vision company, opened an office in Michigan to help drive this manufacturing technology revolution, working with Whirlpool as a key partner. Invisible AI's cofounder Prateek Sachdeva, a University of Michigan graduate, relocated from San Francisco to oversee the tech upgrade.

Another piece of this comeback came together at the Advanced Transportation Center of Washtenaw Community College in Ann

Arbor, where trade workers are being retrained for new technologies in 3D-printed parts; data collection; and smart, connected vehicles. This program is in sync with a state-led push to incorporate Industry 4.0 technologies into half of Michigan's small- to midsized manufacturers by 2025.

In downtown Detroit, I rode the QLINE public transit streetcars to TechTown, an urban business park north of the Edsel Ford freeway, founded in 2000 to support tech spinoffs from Wayne State University and funded by GM and the Henry Ford Health System. It's part of a master plan to reuse historic buildings from the auto-making era in this 149-acre district. TechTown Detroit's president, Ned Staebler, showed me around the five-story startup and coworking hub affiliated with the university, where he doubles as the school's VP of economic development. The technology incubator, originally a service department for Pontiac cars and later the spot where the Corvette was designed, is housed in an industrial structure conceived by the architect Albert Kahn. Nearby, a former Cadillac showroom from 1927, also by Kahn, has been converted into a WeWork space and is the North American headquarters of India's Tata Technologies, with its 150 jobs in engineering and product-development digital services.

TechTown's three metro locations have, since 2007, served 4,500 business owners, who have created 1,600 jobs and leveraged $172 million in startup capital. Two-thirds of the entrepreneurs in its network are African American, in line with the city's demographics. With total venture capital investment coming in at $806 million for Wayne County entrepreneurs,[91] TechTown is an important resource. Smaller hubs are also at work, including the business incubator Green Garage, home to fifty small businesses in an ecofriendly renovated building that dates back to 1920 and was a Model T showroom.

Detroit's comeback has been sparked by several high-profile investors. Native son Dan Gilbert, founder of Quicken Loans, has invested $5.6 billion from his real estate firm Bedrock in a hundred properties and taken the ambitious risk of moving the headquarters of his mortgage company from the suburbs to downtown. Gilbert is the city's largest employer, with 17,000 on payroll. The real estate billionaire developer Stephen Ross has recently seeded a three-building campus with $100 million for the Detroit Center for Innovation, a research and education resource and tech incubator that loops in the University of Michigan and a new anchor tenant from Silicon Valley, digital work-flow company ServiceNow.

This big project is within the fifty-block District Detroit development area, a once-forgotten parcel of land largely owned by the Ilitch family. Entrepreneur Mike Ilitch, founder of the Little Caesars Pizza franchise, has been hailed as a visionary for investing heavily in Detroit and moving his business headquarters from the suburbs to the inner city when others were fleeing. The family holding company owns the Detroit Tigers baseball team, the Detroit Red Wings hockey team, and the iconic Fox Theatre, and it is expanding its shopping and dining outlets. It is also investing in retail, residential, and commercial office developments, as well as a $25 million renovation of the Women's City Club as a hangout for small business owners. Altogether, these new projects in District Detroit (not to mention $40 million for the nearby Mike Ilitch School of Business at Wayne State University) have led to 20,000 construction and related jobs, and a $2.1 billion economic boost.

The flip side of this real-estate frenzy is the huge number of vacant homes still to be demolished—8,000 on top of more than 20,000 torn down since 2014. Blight-reduction efforts have been revamped to prioritize salvageable homes for resale to returning citizens, but the huge job of transforming the city has a long way to go. Detroit's reinvention is still a fragile process, with grittiness mixed in with hip coolness.

It is also a lively city, with no shortage of things to do over a weekend. I watched a Detroit Tigers game at Comerica Park, viewed the Detroit Industry murals by Diego Rivera at the Detroit Institute of Arts Museum, and shopped at Shinola's flagship store, famous for crafting luxury design brands. I also checked out some new mixed-used real estate development projects: El Moore, urban living in a garden setting, and 7.Live, taking the place of a former B. Siegel department store. Even as I left town, I saw flashes of creativity: colorful graffiti, eclectic art installations, facades of derelict houses painted bright orange.

On my way to Dayton on I-75, I made a quick detour to drive through Toledo, Ohio, the "Glass City." The city has a long history of glass manufacturing, which began in 1888 when the New England Glass Company (later Libbey Inc.) chose to relocate here for the abundance of natural gas and high-quality sand and the access to railroads and steamship lines. The city is also the world headquarters for fiberglass and insulation maker Owens Corning and its distinctive campus next to the Maumee River. It's known too as "Jeep Country" for its overhauled plants that today make the popular Wrangler sport utility vehicle and Gladiator pickup.

Downtown, I ran through red lights in the city's concrete shell and torn-up streets under construction, empty during COVID except for panhandlers who approached my car windows. Retail outlets are nowhere to be seen, and boarded-up buildings are numerous. Facing poverty and a high crime rate in concentrated neighborhoods, Toledo fell on hard times and is struggling to deal with the fallout. Facing extensive poverty and a high crime rate, it is searching for a new image of itself, symbolized by a community-led project that has splashed a highly visible mural of daffodils on twenty-eight grain silos along the city's industrial waterfront. Downtown, brighter prospects can be seen in a new convention center and adjoining Hilton hotel complex; rebuilding of a warehouse district with several restaurant newcomers; and a minor league baseball stadium, opened in 2002, which is home field for the Toledo Mud Hens. Then too, there's the fine Toledo Museum of Art, founded in 1901 and generously endowed by Edward Drummond Libbey, regarded as father of the city's glass industry.

The city's signature company, Libbey, recently emerged from bankruptcy and plans to invest $30 million with assistance from state economic organization JobsOhio over the next few years. In return, the company is expected to maintain its glass factory, add a high-end production line, and keep its headquarters in the city, where it employs nearly a thousand. Over the years, the company has outsourced production to plants in China, Mexico, the Netherlands, and Portugal, and tax incentives are now being considered to keep the Libbey operations in Toledo. A setback in the city's rebound came in early 2022, when exercise equipment company Peloton, facing financial challenges, backed out of a pledged $400 million commitment to build its first US factory here and create 2,100 production jobs locally. I stepped on the accelerator, shocked by the scale of deterioration in this former capital of glassmaking but seeing some potential.

The New Dayton

Three hours later I was in Dayton. Despite its innovative heritage, Dayton has also faced tough times: job losses, high poverty, and the exodus of companies like NCR, Mead Paper, Delphi, General Motors, and others, which has cost 50,000 working-class people their jobs since the mid-1980s. Social challenges have loomed large too: a hate-group rally, a deadly mass shooting, and an opioid epidemic.

The metro area is beginning to bounce back economically. GM hired a hundred production and skilled trade workers at a recently opened, $174 million joint venture facility in Brookville making diesel truck engines. This news came after the Chinese company Fuyao Glass bought GM's shut assembly plant in nearby Moraine for $450 million, modernized it, and hired hundreds of hourly workers. The president and CEO, Jeff Liu, oversees about 2,000 Chinese and American workers, nearly as many as GM laid off when the plant shut down in 2008, and Liu has said he will hire another 350 and invest $45 million in expansion. In spite of occasional cultural clashes, Chinese ownership has provided a real economic bonus, and China-to-US investment deals are an intriguing part of the competition between the two superpowers.

I found the surest signs of Dayton's progress toward a new-age economy at the 164-acre site where NCR had been headquartered. Aggregated here are in-depth research and innovation centers by GE Aviation and Emerson Helix, plus an expanded University of Dayton Research Institute, a military R&D powerhouse. Across the street from the former NCR campus, Jeff Hoagland, president and CEO of the Dayton Development Council, was working out of a newly constructed office building. He was well aware that most old-line manufacturing jobs—"dirty, dangerous, and dull"—aren't coming back. "We need to train workers to do higher-end jobs," he said. The council's mission is to increase jobs, building upon the city's two major universities, healthcare institutions, advanced manufacturing, and aerospace markets.

Information technology and cyber businesses in Dayton naturally feed off the Wright-Patterson Air Force Base and Research Laboratory

(AFRL). Bill Harrison, AFRL's director of small business, heads up its innovation research, technology transfer, and commercialization programs. Several midwestern tech startups, including Battle Sight Technologies, have tapped this resource, which seeks, as Harrison has said, to "build bridges between the lab and the community outside the gate." Off base but within sight of it, a retired FBI special agent and former marine corps officer, Timothy Shaw, licensed tech from the AFRL and worked with commercialization experts at the Wright Brothers Institute and at data analytic firm SP Global, where he is a vice president. His most successful spin-off has been GlobalFlyte, a communications technology firm aimed at getting first responders information needed for emergencies.

Dayton's designation as an exclusive air force digital innovation hub should open doors to more collaboration with businesses located "outside the fence," as locals refer to anything off the military base. Other interesting aviation projects are tests of drones for flights below a pilot's sight lines, and research for electric flying cars by Austin-based LIFT Aircraft, partnering with the air force. Also, aircraft maintenance, repair, and overhaul facilities from Sierra Nevada Corporation will bring around 150 new jobs to the birthplace of aviation.

I met Dayton's then-mayor, Nan Whaley, in Courthouse Square downtown, though our conversation was cut short by a rainstorm. As we ran to city hall for cover, folks waved to her, and she smiled and shook hands. Reviving Gem City, as Dayton has been nicknamed for nearly two centuries, had been a focus for the mayor and her path to be Ohio's next governor. Since 2001, $4 billion in public-private investment has poured in to the city, and more recently opportunity zones that offer tax benefits to investors in low-income areas have stimulated reinvestment in tracts covering one-third of Dayton's population and the entire downtown zone.[92, 93]

The reconstruction of its urban core is evidence of the city's can-do spirit. The former Montgomery County Fairgrounds, with $16 million of public-private investment, is being converted into an OnMain complex that includes an innovation and research site, housing units, and parkland. Nearby, the Dayton Arcade complex of five interconnected buildings, dating back to 1902, is being restored after being vacant and unmaintained for twenty-five years. An innovation center at the arcade opened with coworking spaces, a "shark tank" venue, artist lofts, a café, and a conference room. The University of Dayton and the Entrepreneurs' Center signed a joint ten-year lease.

A mile away the warehouse district, called Webster Station, has been refashioned as a technology corridor. The Manhattan Building (so-called because it was used as a research base in developing the atomic bomb) has been rehabbed. New tenants include Battle Sight Technologies and the government contracting software and cyber intelligence company Mile Two, a fast-growth, 110-employee startup that recently won a $15 million air force contract. The tech startup Crowdpurr, which makes interactive apps to engage audiences at events, made its Dayton debut in the district too, bringing the LA-founded startup back home. Its cofounder, Ross Newton, has noted that he's been hiring hard-working local talent cut from the same cloth as himself.

P&G Plus Tech

From Dayton, I continued south on I-75 to Cincinnati. The dual towers of Procter & Gamble's headquarters, where it employs 4,000 of its total of 10,000 staff in the region, stood out on the cityscape. The impact of P&G's leadership and ongoing investment in the city has trickled down to revive the city's most impoverished and dangerous district into an innovation hotspot.

I met P&G's then-treasurer and innovation champion, Valarie Sheppard, in the lobby. "Innovation is the lifeblood of the company. It is like air to us. We've gotten involved in the community as a pace-setter, for a financial return, access to startup innovation, and to help the city. It's a triple win."

We were a long way from the city's identity as Porkopolis, the nick-name Cincinnati once bore as the largest pork-packing center in the world, before the expansion of the railroad shifted the industry west-ward to Chicago. The city's current corporate association with P&G goes back to the immigrants William Procter and James Gamble, who capitalized on the pork industry's fat and oil byproducts to form this soap and manufacturing company in 1837.[94]

Under the leadership of retired CEO Bob McDonald, P&G invested $25 million in 2003 to seed the launch of nonprofit developer 3CDC, which led a city, federal, and community effort to develop blighted areas downtown and clean up the impoverished Over the Rhine district. The historic Music Hall and Memorial Hall were renovated. More shelters were added to reduce homelessness. The 21C Museum, which had been a deteriorating building of federally subsidized apartments, was transformed into an elegant hotel, with a fitness center, rooftop bar, contemporary art gallery, and restaurant. I stayed there during my visit and explored the neighborhood's usually vibrant bars, quaint shops, and restaurants, several closed due to the coronavirus outbreak.

The Over the Rhine neighborhood got its name from the German immigrant workers who settled here in the mid-1800s and crossed the Miami & Eric Canal (now drained) from central downtown to homes a few blocks north. In the mid-1900s, the socioeconomic makeup of the densely populated area began to change. Kentucky and West Virginia mountaineers moved northward to find work as coal mines closed. African Americans relocated here after losing their homes to make way for I 75. The city's manufacturing base of automobiles, steel, and machine tools eroded, and today Cincinnati's population is about two-thirds of its peak in 1950—though it did gain 4.2 percent during the past decade, its first increase in seventy years. The district has now been rebranded as the Digital Rhine.

"We're trying to put Humpty Dumpty back together again," Pete Blackshaw told me. He is a one-time P&G brand manager and entrepreneur who was named CEO of the startup hub and innovation catalyst Cintrifuse in 2018. He previously ran digital innovation for Nestle in Europe. The P&G- and Kroger-supported hub has a flywheel of startup funds, an incubator, a community of entrepreneur members, a coworking and events space, and a unique model of venture investing. Cintrifuse has pooled $120 million of capital into three syndicate funds, including $35 million from P&G, Kroger, and other corporates. These funds are currently invested in eighteen VC firms, including Silicon Valley–connected Refinery Ventures, Upfront Ventures in Los Angeles, and Greycroft Partners in New York. In turn, they've funded more than 700 startups. "We are the great supply way," said Blackshaw, noting the city's building block sectors and an Amazon Air investment of $1.5 billion in a new cargo hub that has added 2,000 jobs.

Another prop to the city's revitalization is a tech agglomeration near the University of Cincinnati. Here, seed investor CincyTech has funded several startups that showcase the city's diverse mix of tech innovations. One is Enable Injections, which developed a yo-yo–sized medical technology device, EnFuse, that lets patients self-administer medications to treat chronic disease. It is backed by $82 million, led by large pharma Sanofi, and a partnership with business software company SAP. Another is Losant, an internet-connected platform for data analytics, which is hiring a hundred workers after raising $14 million. Then there's Astronomer, a software data work-flow startup that's charged up with $68 million in finance, including from several Silicon Valley biggies.

Cowtown No More

After a weekend rest in Lancaster, I was back on familiar Route 33, headed northwest to Columbus. I knew the terrain well going back to the time my mom had showed me around and tried (unsuccessfully) to convince me to move from New York City to the quaint, tree-lined Victorian Village neighborhood near OSU to be closer to home.

Cbus, Columbus's new nickname, remains home to solid but somewhat stodgy retail and foods businesses like the Limited, Borden, and Wendy's—as well as Nationwide Insurance, which has grown over the last century from a small local auto insurance firm to a national powerhouse. And the city continues to be a good test market for new products. The booming field of insurtech, a blend of insurance and technology, is one of many bright spots.

Most people associate Columbus with the Ohio State football team, but Ohio's capital city is seeing a creative spark from new tech in transportation, health, and finance. There's a distinct entrepreneurial vibe. The sporty Arena District, home to the Blue Jackets hockey team and the Clippers baseball team, is a destination for major concerts and good restaurants, from sports bars to the North Market food stalls. To get a feel for the transformation, I stayed for a few nights at the contemporary Canopy Hotel and checked out its rooftop bar, crowded with fashionably dressed young people even on weeknights. The city has seen a 15 percent population surge over the past decade, the largest gain among sizeable midwestern metros. This gain has been increasingly diverse, with a nearly 18 percent increase in African American residents and 75 percent more Asians.

Since winning a national competition led by the US Department of Transportation and $50 million in grants, including from the Paul G. Allen Family Foundation, Columbus has gone all in on mobility innovation—necessary given the clogged highways, although some advancements were paused or discontinued during the pandemic. The Smart Columbus project, as it's been called, has had self-driving shuttles through the city, a downtown Cbus circulator, and the Empower Bus to transport disadvantaged people. Another part of the initiative has been subscription-based microtransit car-sharing services you can schedule in advance. Waymo—formerly the Google self-driving car project—is testing its driverless autonomous vehicles at the Transportation Research Center in the East Liberty neighborhood, where I took a spin. Under the new federal infrastructure law, increased government funding for Amtrak could expand train routes and connect Columbus with Indianapolis, Chicago, and Louisville—a step toward catching up with China's high-speed rail for its major cities. Amtrak passenger train service in Columbus was cut in 1979 due to federal budget cuts and lack of profitability. Sadly, the historic Union Station was demolished (with only the main arch saved) to make way for building a convention center.

Elsewhere, Columbus's legacy industries in healthcare and insurance have become digitized and bulked up. The prescriptions software network CoverMyMeds, which was acquired in 2017 by the healthcare giant McKesson, is building a strikingly modern $240 million corporate campus, eventual home to 1,600 employees. Other healthtech and insurtech companies that have gone public or are about to break out include Olive, Root Insurance, Branch, and Anthemis, among others.[95]

This clump of tech innovation is fueled by the venture capital firm Drive Capital (see chapter 3); spinouts from Ohio State University; the startup studios Rev1 Ventures and Converge Ventures; and inventions at the large nonprofit contract research organization Battelle Memorial Institute, which has pioneered, among many products, the office copy machine, the bar code, and vehicle cruise control.

In recent years, Google and Facebook have broken ground for data centers on a flat, once-agricultural stretch of central Ohio near New Albany, twenty miles northeast of Columbus. Google is investing a further $1 billion to triple its footprint, even buying a 120-acre farm in my hometown of Lancaster. (It's sad to see the cows and corn going away, but this is progress, tech-style.) Though these are big investments, not a lot of workers are needed to run them. There can be other issues. Amazon is opening a data center and adding to its fulfillment and distribution hubs in central Ohio, and neighbors have already complained about the traffic congestion.

In this era of live-work-play places, a master-planned suburban community in New Albany has been developed by Les Wexner, a Columbus native and founder of L Brands. He's been around for a while. My mother and I loved shopping at his Limited store in the once-thriving Eastland Mall, the region's first enclosed shopping center, which lost the last of its four anchor stores in 2017. We also liked driving by the luxurious homes in this new town with its clean, uniform look. The neighborhood of Franklinton, close to downtown, is also benefiting from a master plan that is transforming twenty-one acres of land on the west bank of the Scioto River.

Once full of junkyards and truck storage lots, this neighborhood used to be one that my family avoided when we drove downtown to go shopping at the giant Lazarus department store, unfortunately closed in 2004 after a hundred-year history. Now, nearby Franklinton is hardly recognizable, with several contemporary, mixed-use business and retail operations and the eye-catching Gravity apartment community. The Center of Science and Industry museum, designed by award-winning architect Arata Isozaki, was relocated here in 1999 from downtown, and nearby the dramatic, circular-designed National Veterans Memorial and Museum, envisioned by John Glenn, is an inspirational visiting place.

On to Indy

My visit to Indianapolis included an eight-mile bike tour around town; I pedaled past the state capitol, several museums, headquarters of Eli Lilly, and the White River State Park and canal. It was a great way to see the city. Once a thriving industrial center, a manufacturing and logistics crossroad with rail yards, auto plants, and furniture manufacturers, Indianapolis today has a strong base of diversified businesses that includes the tech multinationals Salesforce and Infosys, the national defense company Raytheon, the pharmaceutical giant Eli Lilly, and the health insurance firm Anthem.

As I mentioned in chapter 1, Indianapolis got on the tech startup map a decade ago when Salesforce acquired ExactTarget and former employees applied their newfound wealth to a range of new tech ventures. This was a sea change. Salesforce moved into the state's tallest building and rechristened it Salesforce Tower, and direct flights to and from San Francisco began. Software-as-a-service (SaaS) became the dominant entrepreneurial activity, aside from home-improvement rating service Angie's List (rebranded Angi). It's a cluster effect like few others. As I described in chapter 3, when Scott Dorsey and his cofounders sold ExactTarget and created the venture studio High Alpha, more SaaS startups flowed from their investment and incubation at High Alpha's offices in the revitalized Bottleworks District, revolving around a 1930s Coca-Cola bottling plant turned into an entertainment hub, a boutique hotel, and a food hall.

Indianapolis's growing tech ecosystem includes a fifty-acre innovation district called 16Tech, initially funded by a $38 million grant from Eli Lilly. The site on the northwestern edge of downtown was still under construction during my visit but has since filled in with a makerspace called Machyne (a makerspace is a community-operated work space where people with common interests can meet and collaborate) and the healthtech startup investor Boomerang Ventures. There is also an artisan marketplace and an innovation hub in the rehabbed former headquarters of the Indianapolis Water Company. This riverfront tech park connects to a local hospital, a university branch, and a range of bioscience research outfits. 16Tech's then-president and CEO, Bob Coy (recently retired), told me he envisions a live-work community of 9,000 within ten years. All of which fits with the city's well-conceived innovation strategy and has helped the population surge by 8 percent to 888,000 over the past decade, led by an influx of young, progressive talent.

Blossoming Biotech

My last stop in Ohio that pandemic summer was Cleveland. The birthplace of Standard Oil and a once-mighty manufacturing center, the city today is known for its medical and biotech prowess. Over its hundred-year history, the world-famous Cleveland Clinic has pioneered medical breakthroughs such as coronary artery bypass surgery and the country's first face transplant. Cleveland's 1,600-acre Health-Tech Corridor is a dynamic cluster of accelerators, business incubators, and 170 innovative companies, altogether attracting 1,800 new jobs and more than $4 billion of investment since 2008.

I learned this history from Baiju Shah, CEO of the Greater Cleveland Partnership, an organization driving the city's emerging economy forward. He told me how Cleveland is marshalling resources to build a knowledge-based economic base, with improved access to high-speed broadband in addition to new smart manufacturing and health-tech firms. Yet, while advanced manufacturing is improving productivity, the payoff in biomedicine technology remains a long way off. Medtech innovation requires years of research, clinical testing, regulatory approval, and funding for product launches. But I saw plenty of it going on during a day-long series of interviews.

My first meeting was with Charu Ramanathan, a successful biotech entrepreneur with a doctorate from Case Western University. In 2006, she founded CardioInsight, which produces a noninvasive mapping system that tracks electrical disorders of the heart. After the company received $42 million in venture and state funding, and then FDA approval, the medical-device manufacturer Medtronic bought the startup for $93 million. Charu became a repeat entrepreneur, cofounding the healthcare service network Vitalxchange.

Next I met Akhil Saklecha, who heads Cleveland Clinic Ventures, created in 2017 to invest in emerging healthcare companies that generate financial returns and tackle massive healthcare problems with, as Akhil put it to me, "moonshot opportunities. What we are looking for is big, bold disruptive developments, and it doesn't have to come from affiliates of any of our institutes." Saklecha had a Silicon Valley pedigree—he had been a partner at the VC firm Artiman Ventures—and it showed. Of ninety companies the firm has launched since 2000, twenty have been acquired, including the healthcare systems data integrator Explorys, purchased by IBM, and MediViewXR, which uses augmented-reality technology and 3D holographic images to guide surgeons. More than $1 billion in equity financing has poured into the clinic's startups.[96]

I received additional insights into Cleveland's biotech status from Len Cosentino, founder of Checkpoint Surgical, which had been spun out of Case Western Reserve University's investment and commercialization firm, Neuro Device Innovations (NDI), known for its groundbreaking work in neuroscience. Since 2008, NDI's healthcare fund, which Cosentino heads, has directed $26 million into potential winners, rounded out by government grants. Its track record includes the $42 million sale of spinoff company SPR Therapeutics to Medtronic in 2008, which returned over 150 times the original investment. Several more potential winners are in the wings.[97]

Like other once-prosperous Great Lakes cities, Cleveland is rebounding from population loss, racial turmoil, declining industry, and pollution (symbolized by the Cuyahoga River blaze in 1969 when floating oil and debris caught fire). Since the 1980s, five Fortune 500 companies departed, including Standard Oil, and between 1970 and 2000, Cleveland's dominant manufacturing base was eroded, accompanied by population loss, high poverty, and declining urban schools.[98] Toward the end of the century, civic leaders banded together to liven up downtown, form economic development groups, and bring in new jobs, such as in the advanced manufacturing sector.

There are success stories outside of medtech and biotech, too. The design studio Nottingham Spirk, creator of the Arm & Hammer Spinbrush, the Swiffer Sweep & Vac, and the Sherwin-Williams Twist & Pour paint container, is now into 3D printing and internet-connected products, thanks to a partnership with EY, a state R&D grant, and a $4 million build-out investment. The company president, John Nottingham, showed me around its converted church headquarters, which has a renovated basement full of 3D printing machines; virtual- and augmented-reality displays; and equipment to design internet-connected products, including an autonomous-driven caddie that walks the golf course.

Pittsburgh—Tech, Not Steel

In the final week of my 2020 Rust Belt tour, I stopped in Pittsburgh. As I mentioned earlier in this book, the city is no longer dependent on steel, iron, and its rivers for competitive advantage; gritty and smelly is giving way to geeky and nerdy. Some people are calling it Roboburgh because of its robotics research and startups, or Silicon Strip because of the tech innovators packed into a narrow, former warehouse district.

Pittsburgh has transformed itself into one of the nation's top research places for technologies of the future. It's a self-driving test bed for Ford and VW-backed Argo AI and Amazon-invested Aurora, as well as Uber's automated driving tech unit, which was acquired by Aurora. It's also an anchor for R&D labs by Facebook, Apple, Google, Zoom, and Intel. In the world of robotics, Pittsburgh is as influential as Boston and San Francisco, according to Joel Reed, executive director of the 100-member-strong Pittsburgh Robotics Network. The fast-growing robotics cluster supports 7,000 jobs, and over the past decade, its robot startups have picked up $3.3 billion in venture capital and private equity, and nearly 600 patents have been filed.[99]

This cluster has led to some intriguing startups, like the self-driving truck convoy Locomation, which I discussed in chapter 3, and the computer-vision road inspector Roadbotics. And it's a home to some exciting research from Robotics Institute faculty member Dr. Jean Oh. She explained to me how she's perfecting algorithms for quick, accurate recognition of objects in real-time navigation—a way to (someday) avoid self-driving accidents.

Pittsburgh's tech status is due in large part to Carnegie Mellon University (CMU), which ranks with Stanford, Harvard, and MIT as a research university. CMU grew out of a $1 million donation made by steel magnate and philanthropist Andrew Carnegie to form Carnegie Technical Schools in 1900. It expanded as Carnegie Tech and merged in 1967 with the Mellon Institute, a science research center. Today, this union of two steel barons has given rise to a world-class leader in computer science, robotics, and artificial intelligence technologies. Alumni even have their own angel investor group: 99 Tartans, which supports fellow graduates.

AI was invented at CMU more than half a century ago, part of what prompted the robotics revolution, which in turn led to driverless vehicles. CMU has cornered robotics: It founded the world's first doctoral program in robotics in 1988 and established the Robotics Institute and National Robotics Engineering Center (NREC). Based in a 100,000-square-foot renovated factory on a six-acre site next to the Allegheny River, NREC is a testing and prototyping center with 160 experts, over 850 individual inventions, and $500 million in funding. Finally, there is the Advanced Robotics for Manufacturing Institute, cofounded by the inventor and professor Howie Choset, who was featured on the *Tonight Show* with his snake-like inspection robot crawling up the leg of host Jimmy Fallon.

The University of Pittsburgh and its School of Medicine also contribute to this sparkling research environment. Jonas Salk tested the polio vaccine here in the mid-1950s, and more than eighty companies with life-changing creations have been spun off from Pitt in just the last five years.

"Our region's rise as a recognized center of tech innovation and excellence is a forty-year overnight success story," Audrey Russo told me. Audrey is the president and CEO of the Pittsburgh Technology Council. We met at a rooftop bar of the Hotel Monaco, the skyline around us framed by towers for the city's corporate giants: Alcoa, PPG, and US Steel. She observed that the city "has been marked by steady, solid gains creating a foundation that appears able to weather most economic shifts. A very different story than the exodus of large-scale steel manufacturers four decades ago." Indeed, the southwestern Pennsylvania region comprises thirteen counties and includes six key high-tech clusters and more than 10,000 technology firms employing nearly 306,000—a quarter of the area's overall workforce.[100]

In Pittsburgh I also spoke with Red Whittaker, one of the world's foremost authorities on robotics and AI and a leader in the effort to teach machines to drive on roads. His pioneering work has also included developing robots that cleaned up the Three Mile Island nuclear accident, acing DARPA's Grand Challenge desert race for robotics vehicles, and competing for the $20 million Google Lunar X Prize for the first privately funded venture to make it to the moon. (No one won and the contest ended in 2018 after ten years.) "Pittsburgh is no slouch," he said authoritatively. "It can invent, create, and build on great technical capabilities. CMU is the big dog in robotics. And space is the next frontier."

Now moonstruck, Whittaker is on the frontier of spacetech. He is the founder of Astrobotic Technology, a lunar logistics startup on a mission to send robot-run inspection rovers to the moon, with plans to deliver payloads or time-capsule items for future generations. The startup team recently secured a $200 million NASA contract to search for ice on the lunar surface, starting in 2024. Like Jeff Bezos and Richard Branson, Whittaker is in the space-race game with Astrobotic and its 130 "astrobots," or employees. When I visited the company, CEO John Thornton, a CMU alum, showed me the lunar landers they have designed, built, and tested, and the control center for trips to the moon, the first since the Apollo missions from 1961 to 1972.

To grasp the new Pittsburgh, you have to know its distinct districts. Once-deserted, now-renovated warehouses make up Robotics Row, a string of well-funded self-driving vehicle startups. The so-called Strip District along a narrow plot of land next to the Allegheny River can still look a bit shabby, but it's getting big-tech neighbors: Facebook's expanded AI labs in a modern four-story office building and the Amazon-invested self-driving tech startup Aurora next door in a renovated warehouse. An old produce terminal has been redeveloped and filled with small businesses, fitness clubs, and dining outlets, as well as the

Table C: The Rust Belt's Recovery: A Progress Check

Columbus
Population: 905,748
2010–2020 % Change: +15.1%
Peak Population: 913,921 (2021)
Poverty Rate: 19.1%
Education: 36.8%

Pittsburgh
Population: 302,971
Peak Population: 675,000 (1950)
2010–2020 % Change: -.9%
Poverty Rate: 19.7%
Education: 45.4%

Indianapolis
Population: 887,642
2010–2020 % Change: +8.2%
Peak Population: 887,232 (2021)
Poverty Rate: 16.9%
Education: 32.1%

Dayton
Population: 137,644
2010–2020 % Change: -2.7%
Peak Population: 260,000 (1960)
Poverty Rate: 29.6%
Education: 18.4%

Detroit
Population: 639,111
2010–2020 % Change: -10.5%
Peak Population: 1.85 million (1950)
Poverty Rate: 33.2%
Education: 16.4%

Flint
Population: 81,252
2010–2020 % Change: -20.7%
Peak Population: 196,940 (1960)
Poverty Rate: 37.3%
Education: 12.3%

Cleveland
Population: 372,624
2010–2020 % Change: -6.1%
Peak Population: 914,808 (1950)
Poverty Rate: 32.0%
Education: 18.6%

Youngstown
Population: 60,068
2010–2020 % Change: -10.3%
Peak Population: 170,000 (1930s)
Poverty Rate: 34.9%
Education: 14.6%

Cincinnati
Population: 309,317
2010–2020 % Change: +4.2%
Peak Population: 504,000 (1950)
Poverty Rate: 24.3%
Education: 38.7%

Poverty threshold for family of four in US is $26,200 for 2020; national poverty rate: 9.4% for adults 18–64.

Education: Bachelor's degree or higher, % of persons age 25 years +

Sources: US Census Bureau, Office of Management and Budget, World Population Review

Wigle Whiskey distillery and restaurant, launched in 2011 by Carnegie Mellon graduate Meredith Grelli as Pittsburgh's first distillery since Prohibition. She treated me to some samples.

In the East Liberty neighborhood, north of CMU's campus, Google is expanding its office space at Bakery Square, where Nabisco was baking cookies and crackers until 1998. Now, engineers and software developers work on computer vision, machine learning, and search systems for shopping—as well as facial recognition technology for Android phones.

The heart of the city's innovation hub is the university area of Oakland, where I stayed at Marriott's recently opened Oaklander Hotel and enjoyed meeting others at its outdoor plaza, next to the tenth-floor bar and dining area. Dave Mawhinney, whom we met in chapter 3 and who directs startup founders into CMU's orbit,[101] told me: "I think the real tipping point for Pittsburgh was 2005, when Google established a remote engineering office here. We've just seen almost every large tech company—Amazon, Apple, Facebook, Facebook Oculus—all establishing a technology and product development base here, which has created an environment where technical entrepreneurs can take risks. If they leave their job today to try something innovative and it fails, they can get a job. We're in a great place right now because we have the critical mass of technology."

What's missing for Pittsburgh to emerge as a counterpart to Silicon Valley? Mawhinney made the point that Pittsburgh's big traditional companies—PPG, Alcoa, US Steel, and Kraft Heinz—are not buying new technologies from local startups. They turn instead to New York, Boston, Atlanta, or the West Coast for their first customers. For emerging tech companies, he said, "the cost of customer acquisition and the time invested is way higher than it should be. If we get more risk capital based here and improve access to the city via our airport, we can get more participation of the mid-to-large corporations here in the innovation ecosystem, and we can sustain the Pittsburgh story as we've seen it evolve." He added, "Perhaps the most unexpected benefit of the growth of the technology industry in Pittsburgh has been our rise from a greasy-spoon-restaurant town to a five-star-restaurant town."

That's certainly one kind of endorsement! And actually, it's not just true of Pittsburgh but of many of the Rust Belt cities I visited. After all, lifestyle quality is important in catalyzing a transition and attracting folks who will experiment with new ways of doing things. I remember when it was hard to find any place to eat but fast-food chains here, and it wasn't that long ago. The Midwest is still a hamburger-and-fries kind of place, but organic and vegetarian and ethnic foods are creeping in, a symbol of different cultures blending in and changing the character of the region. It's not like Silicon Valley, and never will be, but that's not the point. It is gaining sufficient momentum now as a tech-inventive region to rise on its own accord, largely through leveraging assets right in its own backyard.

Chapter Eight

Bricks and Pillars

*How state-led government funding and entrepreneurial services
are jump-starting the region*

Perhaps surprisingly, the earliest success in Ohio's Tech Belt resurgence was not funded by private venture capital but by a state-backed venture development firm in Cleveland called JumpStart. In 2010, this venture hybrid invested $500,000 in the Columbus-based health software startup CoverMyMeds, and in seven years' time the medical technology giant McKesson had bought it for $1.4 billion.

It was a stunning success, and when I met JumpStart's CEO, Ray Leach, during the summer of 2020, he made it plain he was keen to repeat it. "Now the challenge is to do that over and over again," he told me. We were at a casual dinner reception held on the patio of a brasserie in Cleveland. Joining us were the Cuyahoga County executive, Armond Budish, and several local entrepreneurs.

JumpStart, I learned, had invested more than $61 million in 125 Ohio tech startups. My conversation with the group was a good introduction to this different VC model—government-led investing and collaboration with entrepreneurial services that jump-starts tech innovators. Hardly the Sand Hill Road conventional approach, but one that was working for Ohio.

The live-streaming company BoxCast was one of the beneficiaries. Its CEO and cofounder, Gordon Daily, collected $230,000 from JumpStart to launch his platform in 2013. Raising more proved a challenge. He pitched Northern California firms but came back empty-handed. As the startup kept growing and its webcasts took off in late 2020, he secured $20 million in funding, led by Updata Partners in Washington, DC. Now, he's looking to double his team in Cleveland. It was a long and lonely road, but it would have been a dead end without JumpStart in the beginning.

Lack of capital and a still-developing entrepreneurial culture have been drawbacks throughout the region. The kind of government support that JumpStart offers for coaching and funding can help to fill the gaps, particularly in the neediest places where financing alternatives are slim, and entrepreneurs are finding their way. As Bill Nemeth, director of JumpStart's mentoring program, told me, "Somewhere along the way, we lost the DNA of the giant businesses in steel, oil, and rubber, such as Goodyear, Firestone, and Standard Oil. We don't have teams spinning out of Google wanting to be entrepreneurs. The people are not big- or bold-enough thinkers to expand their horizons, are not pushing the boundaries enough to have success of a nation-wide standard." He acknowledged that capital is beginning to flow into the region from the coasts based on some "singles and doubles" successes. But he's still waiting for the "grand slam."

Ohio has a long history of legendary entrepreneurship, from Rockefeller to the Wright Brothers to Harvey Firestone, Benjamin Goodrich, and many others. For a century or so, the oil, steel, and rubber industries established by these businessmen made the state a global leader. But as my trip through the heartland had confirmed, the undoing of that success over the last fifty years had been devastating. Coming across survivors like Goodyear—which still makes racing tires in Akron and keeps innovating new products—had been heartening, but what my trip really told me was that the future depended on new industries springing up to replace the titans of yesterday.

State governments allocating resources and encouraging development of new technologies can be a great starting point for the creation of this future. It is the glue, the foundation that keeps it all together

Table D: Entrepreneurial Services Providers (ESPs) and Job Creators in Ohio and Their Impact

CincyTech, Cincinnati
Portfolio Companies: 80+
Jobs Created: 1,225
Capital under Management: $51 million
Capital Invested: $65 million
Portfolio Companies Attracted Co- and Follow-On Investment: $1.1 billion
Number of Exits: 14
Funds: 5
Cumulative Regional Economic Impact: $1.8 billion in imported capital, revenue, and investment returns (2007–2019)

Rev1 Ventures, Columbus
Portfolio Companies: 100+
2021 Jobs Created and Retained: 955
Capital under Management: $100 million
2021 Investments: $278 million in 27 companies
2021 Value of Startup Exits: $725 million
Funds: Rev1 Fund II, $20 million, 2021 / Future Value Fund, $10 million, 2021 / Rev 1 Ventures, $22 million, 2016
Economic Impact: $4.1 billion (2013–2021), $1.14 billion in 2021 alone, in capital attracted to startups, revenue, and investment returns

The Entrepreneurs' Center, Dayton
Companies Funded: 100
Fund: Ohio Gateway Tech Fund, $10 million, 2021, with Converge Technologies, Sumeru Ventures
Total Third-party Investment in Startups: $35 million+
Capital: As ESP, awarded $2.9 million in 2017, $10.8 million in 2019, $15 million in 2022

JumpStart, Cleveland
Companies Funded: 130+
Capital Invested: $70 million
Jobs Created, JumpStart: 7,399
Jobs Created or Maintained with Collaborative Partners: 10,874
Funds: Evergreen Fund (III), FocusFund, NextFund (II), Healthcare Collaboration Fund
Economic Impact from JumpStart and Partners: $9.1 billion since 2010, $1.2 billion in 2020[102]
Economic Impact from JumpStart: $952 million in 2021

NextTech Ohio, Toledo
Local presence remains but is now powered by JumpStart, using streamlined funding and services for northwest Ohio entrepreneurs.

TechGrowth Ohio, Athens (Ohio University)
Operational Assistance: 555 companies
Seed, Angel, and Services Raised for Tech Startups and Clients over Past Five Years: $315 million+
Preseed Funding: $7 million in 16 startups
Growth Funding: $5 million in more than 100 companies
Economic Activity by Client Companies in 2021: $325 million

JobsOhio, Cleveland

Privatized economic development
organization to bring in new jobs

Funded through profits from sales of
spirituous liquors

Fund: new $50 million evergreen to
invest in fast-growth Ohio tech
companies alongside venture firms,
institutional and strategic investors
in startups, providing matching
capital up to $2.5 million

Investments: 56 companies

Sources: Each program's annual reports, websites, and press announcements

and makes progress possible. State-led funding can prop up new, smaller businesses that the private sector might not favor because of the longer wait for payoffs. And it can partly substitute for still-limited venture capital in the region.

Ohio has been refining this model for some time. In 2002, Governor Bob Taft pioneered the Ohio Third Frontier Commission, a $2.1 billion, tech-based economic development initiative. Funded by taxpayer-backed bonds, it was charged with investing in scalable tech companies and accelerating advancement of strategic high-tech sectors and next-generation jobs. This initiative stood out as an unprecedented, bipartisan effort to move from the smokestack era to an information age.

Since then, the state's economic engine for tech startups has grown to an extensive network of entrepreneurial services providers (ESPs) in six regions. (See table D.) By matching government contributions with private investment, these ESPs capitalize tech startups locally and can be a springboard for small, regional tech-based businesses to grow the economy. Many incubators, accelerators, and research outfits wouldn't exist without this governmental helping hand and the matching funds.

Granted, government and entrepreneurship can be an odd mix. Bureaucracy can clog up the works. When Ohio venture capitalist Mark Kvamme was in an economic development role a decade ago, he criticized the state program for moving slowly in vetting deals, with too few results. By contrast, private venture funds tend to move more swiftly toward big deals, or more easily write off losing deals. At this early point in its transition to tech innovation, the industrial Midwest needs both pistons firing—government and private sector funding.

This is why, as part of an ongoing commitment, Ohio's state-backed Third Frontier Commission doles out funding annually for job-creating technology companies and state-backed startup investors. In 2021, out of $187 million in economic development awards, a big chunk was allocated in revitalization, research, and growth grants, with the bulk going to fourteen regional funds within its state network that seed technology startups in their locale. Over the past ten years, $1.5 billion of Third Frontier investment has poured into these so-called venture hybrids (part government, part private) that have ignited hundreds of startups across the state.[103]

This state support might seem like a lot of money, but it's tiny compared with Silicon Valley–sized funds, which can reach into the billions and arguably are not nearly as impactful. The funding also may not be sustainable.

Startups and venture groups risk overdependence on government checks, which can't be counted on as a steady, year-after-year source. For instance, the bond-supported Ohio Third Frontier pool of $1.2 billion, approved in 2010, has been in jeopardy of not being renewed. An additional $25 million was earmarked in mid-2021 to support five entrepreneurial services providers for 2022, and it's conditioned on meeting performance goals.

A *Cleveland Plain Dealer* editorial noted that the Third Frontier program's renewal should be a priority because it's working. "It helps lift Ohio prospects, while luring smart, ambitious people to move here—or stay here." The editorial pointed out that the initiative "has created nearly 15,000 jobs and is securing a seven-to-one return on the public investment."[104]

In my home region of the Appalachian foothills, the public-private partnership TechGrowth Ohio and my alma mater Ohio University recently showed how it's done. TechGrowth seeded Stirling Ultracold, the ultralow-temperature freezer manufacturer and vaccine storage distributor I visited in chapter 3. The Ohio Innovation Fund followed with a $10 million infusion. In mid-2021 the company was acquired by a publicly traded biotech company, Seattle-based BioLife Solutions, in a $258 million deal. The attraction was Stirling Ultracold's eighty patents, growing revenues, and 150 skilled employees in Athens.

Likewise, in the manufacturing-heavy region of northeast Ohio, the economic development group Team NEO is working to create jobs for a regional workforce of two million and a $200-billion-plus economy. It's specifically looking to boost technology adoption on the factory floor. When I met Team NEO's CEO, Bill Koehler, in Cleveland, he told me they were "looking at the emerging technology sectors, not vertically but horizontally to create a road map for smart manufacturing and additive manufacturing." Team Neo has worked on 483 projects since 2015 that could generate 37,000 new jobs throughout eighteen counties. Of 42 projects in the current pipeline, half are in advanced manufacturing.

The emerging mid-American tech field depends heavily on such stepping-stones to support the regionwide transition from heavy industry to tech-powered businesses and factories in an effort to prod their economies. All transitioning Rust Belt states face the same issue—a lot of innovation horsepower but too little venture capital. Each place has its own repair model. Not to pick on Detroit, but Motor City's VC pond is still mighty slim pickings, although it's nearly quadrupled from 2014 to $316.5 million in 2020[105] and a new, fourth fund of $22 million by Invest Detroit Ventures builds on the momentum.

Here's where state government support comes in with a helping hand, as in Michigan, which is dealing with the aftershocks of the automotive industry decline and trying hard to bring in new tech factories and startups that can create jobs and spur economic growth. Many variations on a theme such as mentorship, startup contests, and grants exist for these state government funding programs, from InvestMichigan to Ben Franklin Technology Partnership to TechPoint in Indiana. All track their progress carefully to see the results and record the economic results in startup creation and job growth. It is starting to have an impact, as I saw positive changes coming on this Rust Belt road trip.

Afterword

A Heartland Journey

*Can the Midwest become a new frontier to help move
the country forward?*

When I began my heartland journey of exploration, I had no idea it would yield such surprises and unpredictable discoveries. Through new eyes, I observed how Greater Appalachia is evolving into a Silicon Heartland. I rediscovered a region I thought I knew well. My lens today is no longer as "Becky"—my childhood name and the name family back in Ohio still like to call me—but a wiser, more mature Rebecca.

As I journeyed, bittersweet memories flooded in. I remembered Sunday dinners at my grandparents' farm, camping in our VW microbus, hiking at Old Man's Cave in the Hocking Hills, rooming with my sister at Ohio University, marching in the Lancaster High School band, and much more. Driving past familiar sights, I could hear my slight midwestern accent taking on more of a southern sound as I became more relaxed on this trip deep into Appalachia.

Complete strangers treated me like I belonged. But my view of the world was larger after a globe-trotting journalistic career. I had made the choice years ago to venture out for new opportunities when the Appalachian foothills were offering few. Yet the region I left behind is no longer a place to escape, I found. Even Silicon Valley's semiconductor maker Intel is creating thousands of jobs at new plants in central Ohio's wide-open acres—alongside data centers from Google, Facebook, and Amazon. Youthful entrepreneurs run their own start-ups in tech clusters within Pittsburgh, Cleveland, Cincinnati, Indianapolis, Detroit, Louisville, and Columbus. These are developments that were nowhere in sight little more than a decade ago.

But more positive change is still needed. After covering China's tech economy boom and seeing that country emerge as a superpower rival to the United States, I knew how urgent it was to speed up and widen the renewal of the Rust Belt.

What's needed? Bolder government plans, increased private capital funding, and a shift to Silicon Valley–type visionary thinking, for starters. To escalate this rebuild, it's essential to retrain blue-collar laborers for higher-skilled work in new technical fields, increase vocational education in high schools that can lead to practical jobs, and offer more motivators and rewards for pursuing entrepreneurship. Other drivers needed are community-led projects that can restore pride and confidence and a massive cleanup of aged factories, empty warehouses, and outdated shopping malls.

Diversification from past industries that were beaten by overseas competition, lower costs, or automation is a highly important contributor to this uplift. Nearly all business sectors today, from finance to transit to healthcare to manufacturing, can benefit from getting on the tech bandwagon. Moreover, innovations in robotics, 3D printing, biotech, and AI can redefine a city's industrial legacy, as has happened in Youngstown, Pittsburgh, and Cleveland.

Innovation tends to occur in clusters and can build in the toughest, most unexpected places, often out of necessity. Silicon Heartland is here now, but it's a long way from powerful Silicon Valley and Silicon Alley. To propel a turnaround of the former Rust Belt, there has to be a decentralization of venture capital. As I noted earlier, most US venture capital investment goes to just three states, and less than 10 percent of the nation's total spending goes to the inland hubs I toured. Support from the federal government or state- and city-supported economic development isn't enough to make up for this shortage.

Yet America's old industrial belt is just getting into the startup groove. Experienced venture players from Silicon Valley are arriving to invest in heartland cities. But it will take more midwestern tech successes before an investment herd charges in. Concentrating more funding of startups from Detroit to Pittsburgh can counter China's national push that reaches their showpiece cities, Shanghai and Chengdu. As anyone who has traveled to China knows, the country's transportation and digital infrastructure is a marvel, in stark contrast to America's decaying bridges, highways, rails, and airports, and its uneven internet and mobile service. The worst of it is in the former Rust Belt. This needs fixing, we know, but let's get on with it.

Reshoring assembly line work from China to the Midwest is another workable solution that can improve the Rust Belt's prospects and increase employment. The pandemic and supply shortages of recent years made clear that the United States needs to lessen its dependence on overseas sources. But reshoring needs to be coupled with retraining of blue-collar workers who can't get by with jobs in the retail sector. This retraining is essential for another reason: today's factories run on automation, artificial intelligence, robotics, and the Internet of Things.

Rosemary Coates, founder and executive director of the Reshoring Institute in Mountain View, California, has put it this way: "The gross, dirty, smelly jobs of the 1960s are not coming back. That's not what manufacturing looks like today. It's about computing and automation and a trained, sophisticated workforce."

It's critical that the country addresses these economic challenges now to maintain its superpower status. Competition between China and the United States for technology innovation leadership has heated to the point of harsh conflict. China has been catching up to the United States for years with state-led blueprints and private funding to advance economically. The China machine has cranked out technologies for electric vehicles, commerce, 5G communications, robotics, biology, and finance. It's also advanced in core tech such as semiconductors and in futuristic sectors of AI, space, and quantum computing.

Having dominated the domestic Chinese market and blocked the advance of America's top digital brands in their home market, China's tech innovators have expanded internationally and broadened their sphere of influence in Southeast Asia and Africa. This outward push reached Silicon Valley—and Wall Street too—before regulatory crackdowns in the past few years halted Chinese investment in many security-sensitive American businesses and technologies and also reduced the number of China IPOs in New York.

China's swift catch-up in technology and R&D underscores the urgency for the United States to tackle the challenges of rebuilding the Rust Belt and revitalizing its research and manufacturing base. China now files 25 percent of global patents, while America's share has declined to 21.5 percent.[106] China's share of R&D spending globally has reached 22 percent of the total, gaining on 27 percent for the US.[107] In venture capital, the trends tellingly follow this pattern. The US share of VC spending globally has slipped from 84 percent in 2004 to just below 50 percent today.[108] China has increased venture spending from $5.6 billion in 2010 to $106.4 billion in 2021 (second to US VC spending of $329 billion). In 2018 China VC spending surged, almost surpassing US totals.[109] ByteDance, the Chinese maker of TikTok, is the world's most valuable privately funded company, worth $140 billion.[110] Need I go on?

Building a Better Mousetrap

The United States has led virtually every major technological advance of the last century, from planes to computers to rockets to television to telephony to atomic weapons. But without action, America's global tech lead will not hold. Many in Congress understand this, and the House and Senate's passing of versions of the Endless Frontier Act have been a welcome response, promising to supercharge America with federal funding of cutting-edge science and technologies to combat China's increasing challenge and outcompete the world in industries of the future. That momentum can be enhanced by empowering high-tech economies in emerging frontier hubs that were left behind by the closure of factories and mines. The tech boom largely bypassed Middle America. As this book has shown, that gap is being addressed, and a frontier plan calling for the creation of regional technology hubs to foster innovation well outside the traditional coastal strongholds would be equally welcome.

Now that the United States and China are caught up in a tech superpower race,[111] the days of Chinese buying into America's Rust Belt to keep factories humming are gone. Direct investment from China has dwindled to $7.2 billion from a peak of $45 billion in 2016,[112] when the Chinese tech titans Baidu, Alibaba, and Tencent invested heavily in Silicon Valley startups. High-profile deals like the Chinese purchase of a former GM plant in Ohio, which I discussed in chapter 7, would be highly unlikely today.

With a united effort, committed business leaders, emboldened entrepreneurs, open-minded venture investors, community connectors, and state-run economic growth organizations can restore America's backbone. Pumping up the frontiers of the Midwest can even out opportunities, bring back jobs, raise incomes, ease social unrest, and keep America's economic engines going while China races ahead and threatens to grab the lead. Given the enormity of our country's challenges, President Biden's "blue collar blueprint to build America" and pledge "to grow the economy from the bottom up and middle out" sound promising.

This push builds on America's pioneering, adventuresome spirit, which breeds risk taking, inventiveness, and bold self-starters—nearly impossible to copy. It could very well be true: as goes the Rust Belt and my home state, so goes the nation.

The Old Home Place

The travels I took for this book made me realize that, with the right resources and willpower, a society and its economy can change for the better in just a generation or two. I've observed how a Silicon Heartland has been gradually forming in the years since I left the Midwest—an awareness helped by my experience in Silicon Valley and emerging hubs in faraway lands as well as an understanding of my homeland's culture. As I consider how this development will grow in the future, I'm hoping that the heartland's special values of hard work, family tradition, kindheartedness, and pride will be retained. This hope became clear to me on the final part of my odyssey, when I went to see the Fannin family homestead, on Zion Ridge in eastern Kentucky.

My homeward-bound journey, with my husband along with me for this last part of the trip, began in the northern Kentucky town of Quincy on the Ohio River, just over the Ohio-Kentucky border. The town is so tiny the only building in sight was a post office. I pulled over and parked to ask the postal clerk for directions, since my GPS wasn't much help in this remote countryside. A fellow who was picking up his mail (it's no longer delivered in this area, given cutbacks) racked his brains and came up with some sketchy directions. Venturing out, I got a mile along the dusty road he suggested when I saw his pickup in my rearview mirror. He was following me because he'd forgotten to tell me that a bridge was out up ahead. This complete stranger kindly led me on a detour to a different route.

That road took me to a higher elevation. The tires started kicking up gravel. Every once in a while, I'd pass a trailer home where dogs sometimes snapped at my wheels. Nearing the top of the hill, I passed Granny Thomas Cemetery. Another curve of the road and I passed Logan Cemetery. At the peak, a straightaway afforded a view of distant forests, blue skies, and puffy clouds.

I hadn't seen another car for miles, but suddenly one appeared, traveling slowly. I passed it and kept going until I spotted a road sign for Zion Ridge. The other driver pulled his car in right behind mine. This being friendly territory, I rolled down my window, and we exchanged hellos. I mentioned I was searching for my ancestral home and asked the couple inside if they had any idea where it could be on this dirt mountain road. They did! We got out of our cars to chat and began exchanging names and places. Timothy and Jennifer were on a road trip from their home in North Carolina to visit the Kentucky countryside of his childhood. Amazingly, it turned out that he had grown up in the same house my great-grandparents had owned a generation before.

Timothy, a salt-of-the-earth character and a storyteller, talked up a storm about his childhood home. "You have to understand, there was no running water. We took baths in the nearby pond. It's also where the cows drank water," he told me. "There was no outhouse, either. When the hole filled up, we moved on and dug another hole," he said. Wolves and bears roamed the property at night. Was this a tall tale?

Hard to tell, but I wasn't about to camp out here, as Timothy claimed he had many times. His story was heartfelt, with no hint of shame from growing up poor on this ridge. Why would there be, from a heartland perspective?

Sadly, I learned from him that the old home place was gone, burned down in a fire just a few years earlier. As we continued to share memories, a pickup truck carrying a load of hay pulled up. We told the driver about my homeland search, and naturally he knew the way. His family name was Riffe, same as the cemetery that overlooks the Fannin lands. We're distant relatives by marriage; my great-uncle Asa Fannin married Mondain Riffe. Hearing this, Timothy piped up, adding that his mother had married a Riffe. This was definitely getting very hillbilly. What was the chance that we'd all end up at this same spot at the same time? Yet there we were, bonding across the years and the many divides.

At the entrance to the cemetery was a sign that read *Gone for now, but loved forever*. Sitting in the rolling hills was a picturesque red barn, where tobacco leaves had been hung out to dry. There was also a cattle pasture. My mind wandered back twenty years, when I came here on a visit with my mom, brother, and some Fannin relatives. It was on that trip that I'd learned some family history.

My great-grandfather, Sherman Fannin, married Sarah Hutchinson in 1899, and they made Zion Ridge their home in the 1920s. My grandparents Cecil and Anna Fannin moved in with them during the Great Depression, after Cecil lost his job at Goodyear Tire & Rubber in Akron, Ohio. As the oldest son, he was put in charge of the farm, with his brother Asa and cousin Renford. Sherman was very religious and would leave home for weeks at time, following evangelists who had passed through. Cecil, Asa, and Renford never got over feeling deserted. On the farm they grew tobacco, logged the white oak timber, and raised cattle. They rode horses nine miles each way to pick up supplies from the country store and deliver the logs by mule to be made into railroad ties.

As my mother recollected after that trip, "Your grandfather Fannin never talked about these things in my presence. A big vacuum was filled for me. I think that your dad would have benefited if he'd allowed himself to learn about it. For some reason he didn't like talking about his past." My dad, like his father, had known these humble beginnings. His intellect and ambition guided him out of his rural past to a doctoral degree in history. My entrepreneurial grandfather flew his own plane, traveled to his Florida home each season in his RV to go fishing at Lake Okeechobee, bought a new Cadillac every year, and owned two hardware stores in southeastern Ohio. My father and he did not get along.

Leaving this homestead, an unforgettable incident happened when the brakes on my car started grinding and almost stopped working. This being the heartland, a mechanic who was working on a Saturday afternoon in July didn't complain at all as he put new brake pads on my vehicle in just an hour, and charged me only $110. Having my husband, John, along for this homeland journey gave me an additional perspective. Appalachia was unfamiliar terrain for him. As he explained to his brother Ken in an email after the trip, "Growing up in New York City, we always had a rather arrogant attitude about anyone who wasn't from Manhattan, or even just the Upper East Side, but Rebecca has broadened my cultural horizons and exposed me to the heartland. People are helpful and friendly and not obsessed with the almighty dollar. Family and friends are important. Total strangers chatted with us and helped us out. The whole area was a bit like [the TV show] Mayberry," where everyone knows everybody and where not much has changed since 1930.

But of course as my travels—and this book—have shown, it is changing. As I have changed. When my parents drove me from Lancaster to New York City in the late 1970s, after my college graduation, I remember my mom saying that I had searched hard to find something better than where I grew up. And by leaving for the big city when I did, I did duck the job losses and drug addiction crisis that ravaged the Rust Belt well into this century (though I was in Manhattan starting a new job on that awful 2001 day of the 9/11 terrorist attack). Yes, my horizons broadened and experience deepened. Yes, I also missed those things that make the Midwest great, the people and values and countryside that has always made this wonderful region the heartland. The *heart* of America. So to return as I did and to find it being revitalized and growing in so many ways—reinventing itself without losing its great virtues—wasn't just an education for me. It was personally satisfying. I was returning home, and home was returning to the vibrant industrial landscape it once was, but with twenty-first-century industries.

To prosper, places like where I grew up need to keep talent from moving away for seemingly greener pastures. Now, thanks to a spreading Silicon Heartland in the Rust Belt, a new generation of millennials and Gen Zers don't need to leave home; they can "build a better mousetrap, and the world will beat a path to" their door. Greater diversity, open-mindedness, and creative energy are driving these changes in places where, up until recently, not much changed, except for the worse.

The foothills of the Appalachians are still a large part of who I am and always will be. And they are also a large part of what America is. It's been an amazing journey so far, with many more crossroads to navigate, both for myself and the region as a whole, and looking ahead, I realize there's no turning back. Every major holiday, I drive to Ohio—for Christmas Eve candlelight service at the Presbyterian Church, the July 4 parade and fireworks at the county fairgrounds, barbeque cookouts with home-grown vegetables straight from the garden, and lots of laughs with my siblings in Lancaster. My hope is that the progress I saw on my amazing journey through the heartland will continue to expand, and that my future visits will see this great region continue to rise again.

Appendix A

A Snapshot of Midwest Venture Capital Anchors

High Alpha

Location: Bottleworks district, Indianapolis

Launched: 2015

Managing Partner: Scott Dorsey

Funds: 3 totaling $216 million, with the third at $110 million in 2021

Investments: 76

Investment sectors: B2B SaaS

Geographic Focus: Indiana

Notable Deals: Lessonly (acquired); Attentive, ($900 million from Softbank, Coatue, Tiger Global); LogicGate ($145 million from Jump Capital, SVB); and Zylo ($35 million from GGV Capital, Menlo Ventures, Bessemer Venture Partners)

Notable Backers: The Foundry Group in Boulder and Emergence Capital in San Francisco

Allos Ventures

Location: Indianapolis

Launched: 2010

Cofounder & Managing Partner: Don Aquilano

Funds: 3, third fund of $52 million in 2020
Investments: 23
Investment sectors: Software and tech-enabled business services
Powers: Sixty8 Capital for investing in diversity-led startups
Geographic Focus: Indianapolis and surrounding Midwest
Notable Deals: Lessonly, Scale Computing

Magarac Ventures

Location: Pittsburgh
Launched: 2021
Cofounders: Draper Triangle colleagues Jay Katarincic, Zach Malone, Mike Stubler, plus Will Allen; Jeff Wilke, former CEO of Amazon's worldwide consumer business is a strategic adviser and investor
Funds: $40 million toward $150 million initial fund
Rebranded from Draper Triangle
Investment Sectors: software, robotics, medical devices
Geographic Focus: Pittsburgh, Columbus, Ann Arbor, Cleveland, Cincinnati, Detroit

Draper Triangle

Location: Pittsburgh
Launched: 1999
Managing Directors & Cofounders: Jay Katarincic, Mike Stubler
Funds: 3 totaling $210 million
Investments: 60
Investment Sectors: robotics, big data analytics, software, mobile apps, medical devices, IoT connected devices
Geographic Focus: Pittsburgh area, Detroit, Columbus
Notable Deals: fintech platform Alviere (pivot from digital payment app Mezu); banking solution Autobooks ($5.5 million in 2017); AI digital collaborator Aware (led $3 million in 2017, coinvested $12 million in 2020); health plan software maker Babel Health (co-led $5 million in 2019); tech-enabled real estate rental firm Ikos ($4 million in 2019); and autonomous driving truck convoy Locomation (coinvested $5.5 million in 2018 and $10.4 million in 2020)

Acquisitions: Oracle paid $500 million for field sales management software Toa Technologies in 2014. Medtronic purchased medical device maker CardioInsight Technologies for $93 million in 2015.

Mountain State Capital

Location: Morgantown, West Virginia, and Pittsburgh
Launched: 2018
Partners: Michael Green, Matt Harbaugh
Fund: $20 million
Investments: 20
Sectors: Diverse mix of tech startups
Geographic Focus: Greater Appalachia region
Notable Deals: Ride-sharing and delivery tracker Gridwise; parking meter app MeterFeeder; Locomation; skincare solution Serucell
Notable Backers: former Oracle CEO Ray Lane, Huntington Bancshares, SBIC (US Small Business Investment Administration)

Ohio Innovation Fund

Location: Columbus
Launched: 2016
Managing Director: Bill Baumel
Fund: $40 million
Investments: 23
Geographic Focus: Midwest, with Ohio focus
Notable Deals: biopharma device Enable Injections; prescription delivery and medicine reminder service ScriptDrop; ultracold freezers Stirling Ultracold; and eFuse, a LinkedIn of the e-sports business
Backers: OU, OSU, and Kent State

Appendix B

Variations on Startup Support by State

Kentucky

- Innovation investment program provides microgrants and professional services to help startups navigate how to win and manage federally funded small-business research grants and tech transfers
- Deploys startup support capital through Kentucky Enterprise Fund
- Extensive commercialization program combines higher education institutions and the Kentucky Science & Technology Corporation (KSTC), which operates innovation programs and makes investments in tech startups
- Launched New Blue Ventures to amplify investment resources and manage capital for startups working closely with Blue Grass Angels and KSTC
- Amplify Louisville and Endeavor round out the entrepreneurial ecosystem with startup and founder networking and services to launch products

Indiana

- State's nonprofit tech industry accelerator TechPoint runs well-supported Mira annual awards, which honor entrepreneurs and venture investors

- Next Level Indiana fund of $250 million invests in venture capital firms
- Elevate Ventures, Indiana's venture development program, has invested $120 million in 428 startups, attracted $1.2 billion in private coinvestment, and matches funds from Small Business Innovation Research and Small Business Technology Transfer program for startups
- Preseed program awards grants of $5,000 to $25,000

Michigan

- InvestMichigan houses $300 million series of funds to grow next generation of companies
- Venture Michigan runs fund-of-funds totaling $95 million to invest in Michigan startups and diversify the economy
- Invest Detroit Ventures' first evergreen fund for the state pools up to $35 million to seed fast-growing tech startups
- Michigan Economic Development Corporation spearheads creation of Industry 4.0 accelerator to provide funding and coaching for startups to tap into and adopt robotics, 3D printing, and augmented reality for the factory

Pennsylvania

- Ben Franklin Technology Partners
- Economic development program has invested in more than 4,500 technology-based companies and helped to generate 148,000 jobs since its start in 1983
- Budgeting another $14.5 million in funding innovation investments through 2022
- Limited-partner investor in two of city's startup investors: Draper Triangle and Innovation Works, the main nonprofit and most active investor in southwestern Pennsylvania startups
- Innovation Works launched in 1999 and has invested $117 million-plus in 730 tech startups and helped to catalyze $3.3 billion in follow-on investment from more than 100 venture capital firms in major financial and technology centers across the country in IW's portfolio companies[113]

Sources: Each program's annual reports, websites, and press announcements

Acknowledgments

My thanks to all those entrepreneurs, venture investors, and community leaders I interviewed during the height of the COVID outbreak. While some interviews were done over Zoom, most took place in person in their own locale. As I made the rounds from Pittsburgh to Cleveland to Detroit to Indianapolis and beyond, my notebooks filled with their memorable stories of overcoming hardship with hard work, determination, and creativity.

Special thanks to my book editor, Kevin Stevens, who understood the concept, made the text sing, future-proofed the content, and made sure all the elements fit together well, working with the highly capable team at Imagine Books. As he humbly said when I thanked him, "That's my job." To my book agent, Leah Spiro, thanks for being a guiding light and continuing to cheer me on, now on this heartland journey. It's been a productive fifteen years of working together, with three prior books plus this one now.

Silicon Valley tech icons John Chambers, Ray Lane, and Brad Smith gave generously of their time to offer insights about the region's prospects for a comeback, aside from their own contributions to moving Appalachia forward. All three appeared as featured guests on my online show, Ask a VC Anything! So did Bloomberg Beta's venture investor Roy Bahat, whose firm has led VC tours of comeback cities.

Local, state, and national politicians, including congressmen Ro Khanna of Silicon Valley and Tim Ryan of Ohio, took time from busy schedules to do interviews with me about what it will take to revitalize the former Rust Belt. So did mayors from several cities: Bill Peduto from Pittsburgh, Nan Whaley from Dayton, Jamael Tito Brown from Youngstown, Sheldon Neeley from Flint, and of course David Scheffler from my hometown of Lancaster.

Let me thank all the technology innovation leaders and entrepreneurial community builders in transitioning Rust Belt cities who helped to guide my journey. In Pittsburgh, Rachel Burcin of Carnegie Mellon University, Kit Mueller of RustBuilt, and Audrey Russo of Pittsburgh Technology Council led the way. In Cleveland, Baiju Shah of the Greater Cleveland Partnership introduced me to the city's thriving biotech small businesses while Ray Leach of JumpStart and county executive Armond Budish illustrated how economic development organizations are pushing startups forward. In Detroit, Otie McKinley of the Michigan Economic Development Corp. and Ned Staebler of TechTown showed me what it means to start from Rust Belt roots and move into high tech. In Flint, investor and developer Phil Hagerman of Skypoint Ventures introduced philanthropy and good citizenship as driving forces in the city's revitalization with his numerous redevelopments to build entrepreneurship. In Youngstown, Barb Ewing and Jim Cossler of the Youngstown Business Incubator toured me around their five-building campus specializing in 3D printing technologies. In Indianapolis, Cheryl Reed of TechPoint demonstrated how a cluster effect is helping Indy gain a reputation as a startup hub. In Dayton, Shannon Joyce Neal of the Development Coalition and Scott Koorndyk of the Entrepreneurs' Center proved what a difference two decades can mean in a medium-sized city undergoing a renaissance. In Cincinnati, Pete Blackshaw of community investor Cintrifuse clued me in to two corporate leaders of innovation—P&G and Kroger—in Cincy's progress. In Columbus, Jennifer Fening, a leader of the city's jobs and economic development, got me plugged into Smart Columbus and its mobility project, while Eric Wagner of Converge Ventures connected me with the state's economic development organizations. In Louisville, Larry Horn of Amplify, Jackson Andrews of Endeavor, and Tony

Ellis then at KY Innovation held a roundtable with several entrepreneurs and me to discuss local startup trends. In Portsmouth, the late Jeremy Burnside sent me dozens of clippings about the city's comeback spirit and showed me his buildings and others under renovation, walking the town with community leaders Sean Dunne and Tim Wolfe. At my alma mater of Ohio University in Athens, Stacy Strauss of the Innovation Center and TechGrowth Ohio described the state's southeastern road map for success and introduced one of its startup stars in the Appalachian foothills. In West Virginia, at Marshall University, then-president Jerome Gilbert and Dean Avi Mukherjee personally took me on a tour of the campus and startup incubation center and described their entrepreneurial curriculum. At West Virginia University in Morgantown, Sarah Biller of accelerator Vantage Ventures highlighted how the accelerator Vantage Ventures she runs is helping to lead the Mountain State forward with more startups right on campus.

Many venture investors on my itinerary met with me and provided additional insights about startup funding, which is so core to the region's comeback. They include Mark Kvamme and Chris Olsen of Drive Capital; Steve Case of Revolution; Scott Dorsey of High Alpha; Don Aquilano of Allos Ventures; Jay Katarincic, Zach Malone, and Will Allen of Magarac Ventures; Scott Shane and Patrick McKenna of Comeback Capital; Dami Osunsanya of SoftBank Opportunity Fund; Mike Venerable of CincyTech; Tim Schigel of Refinery Ventures; Tom Walker of Rev1 Ventures; Bill Baumel of Ohio Innovation Fund; Ernie Knight of Valley Growth Ventures; Rich Lunak of Innovation Works; Mike Green and Matt Harbaugh of Mountain View Capital; and Carnegie Mellon's Dave Mawhinney.

Thanks to hospitable lodgings, several extended stays on my journey gave me a chance to absorb the culture of each place. Let me thank Shinola Hotel in Detroit, the Oaklander and Kimpton's Hotel Monaco in Pittsburgh, Alexander Hotel in Indianapolis, Canopy Hotel in Columbus, DoubleTree in Youngstown, Detroit Foundation, Hyatt Regency in Cleveland, Marriott hotels in Morgantown and Huntington, Lytle Park Hotel in Cincinnati, and 21C Museum Hotel in Louisville, Lexington, and Cincinnati.

Special thanks to my brother Kyle and sister-in-law Kelly for welcoming me back home in Lancaster, Ohio, with a comfortable place to rest up several weekends during my travels. Not only that, but they read the manuscript and helped to keep me up to date with local insights and news. Big thanks to my husband, John, who accompanied me on parts of the lengthy road trip and offered a running commentary from a New York perspective—plus, he took many photos. He also read through versions of the manuscript and provided a historical point of view. I also want to thank writer and brother-in-law Ken for his feedback to an early draft that helped me frame the storyline. My sister Deborah, a workaholic like me, kept me motivated from Chicago as my writing and research went on and on. Cousin Judy related memories from growing up on the family farm at Gampp Lane, where she still spends holidays. Fannin-side relatives steered me to an unforgettable trip to the Zion Ridge homestead in Kentucky.

Finally, my Honda Element kept going nearly 8,000 road miles of this journey—only needing a brake pad repair and an oil change. It is still my trusty way of getting around, now nearing 80,000 miles.

Endnotes

1. Allison Levitsky, "Bay Area Tech Workers Reveal if They've Left the Region Since Covid19," *Silicon Valley Business Journal* (August 5, 2020), https://www.bizjournals.com/sanjose/news/2020/08/05/poll-finds-that-15-of-bay-area-tech-workers.html.
2. Colin Yasukochi, "2021 Scoring Tech Talent," *CBRE* (July 12, 2021), based on US Bureau of Labor Statistics, April 2021, https://www.cbre.us/research-and-reports/scoring-tech-talent-in-north-america-2021.
3. Aaron M. Renn, *Midwest Success Stories* (Manhattan Institute: November 2019), https://media4.manhattan-institute.org/sites/default/files/midwest-success-stories-aaron-renn.pdf.
4. William H. Frey, *Census 2020*, (Brookings Institution: April 26, 2021), https://www.brookings.edu/research/census-2020-data-release/.
5. Drew DeSilver, "Most Americans Unaware that as US Manufacturing Jobs Have Disappeared, Output Has Grown," Pew Research Center, July 25, 2017, https://www.pewresearch.org/fact-tank/2017/07/25/most-americans-unaware-that-as-u-s-manufacturing-jobs-have-disappeared-output-has-grown/.
6. "Urban Decline in Rust Belt Cities," Federal Reserve Bank of Cleveland, May 20, 2013, https://www.clevelandfed.org/newsroom-and-events/publications/economic-commentary/2013-economic-commentaries/ec-201306-urban-decline-in-rust-belt-cities.aspx.
7. Robert Scott, "Rebuilding the American Economy," Economic Policy Institute, August 10, 2020, https://www.epi.org/publication/reshoring-manufacturing-jobs/.
8. US Energy Information Administration, *Today in Energy*, December 11, 2019; https://www.eia.gov/todayinenergy/detail.php?id=42275.
9. Colin Yasukochi, "2021 Scoring Tech Talent," *CBRE* (July 12, 2021), based on US Bureau of Labor Statistics, April 2021; https://www.cbre.us/research-and-reports/scoring-tech-talent-in-north-america-2021.

10. "IT Industry Outlook 2020," CompTIA, November 2019, https://www.comptia.org/content/research/it-industry-outlook-2020.

11. US Small Business Administration, Office of Advocacy, October 2020, https://cdn.advocacy.sba.gov/wp-content/uploads/2020/11/05122043/Small-Business-FAQ-2020.pdf.

12. "Making It in America, Revitalizing American Manufacturing," McKinsey & Co, November 13, 2017, https://www.mckinsey.com/featured-insights/americas/making-it-in-america-revitalizing-us-manufacturing.

13. John Wu and Robert D. Atkinson, "How Technology-Based Start-Ups Support US Economic Growth," Information Technology & Innovation Foundation, November 28, 2017, https://itif.org/publications/2017/11/28/how-technology-based-start-ups-support-us-economic-growth.

14. US Census Bureau QuickFacts, Flint, Michigan, 2019, April 1, 2020, https://www.census.gov/quickfacts/fact/table/flintcitymichigan/INC110219.

15. US Census Bureau, "Census Bureau Releases New Data on Minority-Owned, Veteran-Owned and Women-Owned Businesses," October 28, 2021, https://www.census.gov/newsroom/press-releases/2021/characteristics-of-employer-businesses.html.

16. US Census Bureau, QuickFacts, Indianapolis, 2019, April 1, 2020, https://www.census.gov/quickfacts/fact/table/IN,indianapoliscitybalanceindiana/PST045219.

17. Bob Gradeck, *The Root of Pittsburgh's Population Drain*, (Carnegie Mellon University Center for Economic Development, November 2003), https://www.heinz.cmu.edu/ced/file/pop-drain.pdf.

18. "Hydroponics Market Worth $16 Billion by 2025," *Bloomberg Business* (May 9, 2019), https://www.bloomberg.com/press-releases/2019-05-09/hydroponics-market-worth-16-0-billion-by-2025-exclusive-report-by-marketsandmarkets.

19. Quick Facts, Ironton, Ohio, US Census Bureau, 2019, https://www.census.gov/quickfacts/fact/table/stowcityohio,irontoncityohio/EDU635219.

20. Heather Stephenson, Community Needs Assessment, Lawrence County, Ohio, Prepared by Ironton–Lawrence County Community Action Organization, 2020 PDF, accessed December 17, 2020. Community Action Partnership Report, Scioto County, Ohio; Data Report 2018; accessed January 18, 2021.

21. Valarie Sheppard retired from P&G in September 2020. She continues to serve on the board of the Federal Reserve Bank of Cleveland and several companies in consumer goods and technology.

22. Smithies is now a partner focused on climate tech investments at Fifth Wall. Episode 7, Mike Otworth, PureCycle, Agile Precision podcast, December 6 week, 2020, https://soundcloud.com/bmwiventures/ep-7-mike-otworth-ceo-purecycle.

23. Regional Economic Data, Eastgate Regional Council of Governments, Mahoning County, Trumbull County, 2019, PDF accessed July 14, 2020, US Census Bureau QuickFacts, Youngstown, Ohio, https://www.census.gov/quickfacts/youngstowncityohio.

24. Remarks made at White House briefing about Lordstown Motors, September 28, 2020, https://www.whitehouse.gov/briefings-statements/remarks-president-trump-congratulating-lordstown-motors-2021-endurance-vehicle/.

25. "Today's Electric Vehicle Market," Pew Research Center, June 7, 2021, https://www.pewresearch.org/fact-tank/2021/06/07/todays-electric-vehicle-market-slow-growth-in-u-s-faster-in-china-europe/.

26. Kevin Adler, "Global Electric Vehicle Sales Grew 21 percent in 2020," *IHS Markit* (May 3, 2021), https://cleanenergynews.ihsmarkit.com/research-analysis/global-electric-vehicle-sales-grew-41-in-2020-more-growth-comi.html.

27. "Slow Start for Electric Vehicles in the US, but Times Are Changing," ING, December 1, 2021; https://think.ing.com/articles/slow-start-for-electric-vehicles-in-the-us-but-times-are-changing.

28. "Electric Vehicle Share in the US Reaches Record Levels in 2020," *HIS Markit* (February 19, 2021), https://news.ihsmarkit.com/prviewer/release_only/slug/bizwire-2021-2-19-electric-vehicle-share-in-the-us-reaches-record-levels-in-2020-according-to-ihs-markit.

29. Sherry Linkon and John Russo, "With GM Job Cuts, Youngstown Faces a New 'Black Monday,'" *Bloomberg CityLab* (November 28, 2018), https://www.bloomberg.com/news/articles/2018-11-27/gm-s-job-cuts-reopen-old-wounds-in-youngstown-ohio.

30. Regional Economic Data, Eastgate Regional Council of Governments, Mahoning County, Trumbull County, 2019, PDF accessed July 14, 2020; US Census Bureau QuickFacts, Youngstown, Ohio, based on 2019–2020 figures, https://www.census.gov/quickfacts/youngstowncityohio.

31. Stephanie Hernandez McGavin, "Can a Defunct Factory Return to Relevance?" *Automotive News* (February 26, 2018), https://www.autonews.com/article/20180226/OEM01/180229895/can-a-defunct-factory-return-to-relevance.

32. Venture Capital Funding Report Q4 2020, PwC/CB Insights Money-Tree Report Q4 2020, January 13, 2021, https://www.cbinsights.com/research/report/venture-capital-q4-2020/.

33. Micah Walker, "Root Insurance Lays Off 330 Employees, Citing Pandemic Challenges," *Columbus Dispatch*, January 21, 2022, https://www.dispatch.com/story/business/2022/01/21/root-insurance-lays-off-330-employees-citing-pandemic-challenges/6606337001/.

34. NVCA 2022 Yearbook, March 2022, https://nvca.org/wp-content/uploads/2022/03/NVCA-2022-Yearbook-Final.pdf. Seven core states in the Rust Belt and Appalachia (Pennsylvania, Ohio, Michigan, West Virginia, Kentucky, Indiana, and Illinois) represent a fraction of national venture capital investment.

35. PitchBook-NVCA Venture Monitor, January 13, 2021, https://pitchbook.com/news/reports/q4-2020-pitchbook-nvca-venture-monitor.

36. *Beyond Silicon Valley*, Revolution and PitchBook report, November 11, 2021, https://revolution.com/beyond-silicon-valley-report/.

37. "America's Mighty Middle Report," Crunchbase, May 12, 2020, https://about.crunchbase.com/mighty-middle-report-2020/.

38. *Beyond Silicon Valley*, Revolution and PitchBook Report, November 11, 2021, https://revolution.com/beyond-silicon-valley-report/.

39. "America's Mighty Middle Report," Crunchbase, May 2020, https://about.crunchbase.com/mighty-middle-report-2020/.

40. "Angel Investors with Investments in the Midwest," Crunchbase, https://www.crunchbase.com/hub/angel-investors-investments-in-midwestern-us-.

41. "Accelerators with Investments in the Midwest," Crunchbase, https://www.crunchbase.com/hub/accelerators-investments-in-midwestern-us-.

42. NVCA 2020 Yearbook, National Venture Capital Association, April 1, 2020; Ohio, Illinois, and Pennsylvania ranked among the top ten states for fund-raising in 2019, while Ohio, Illinois, and Michigan recorded the biggest year-over-year gains in venture capital funds raised.

43. *State of Venture 2021 Report* (CB Insights, January 12, 2022), https://www.cbinsights.com/research/report/venture-trends-2021/.

44. Mae Rice, "The Tech Industry Has Outgrown the Bay Area," Builtin.com America's Mighty Middle Report, July 30, 2020, https://builtin.com/founders-entrepreneurship/mighty-middle-report.

45. *Startup Failure Post-Mortems* (CB Insights, June 17, 2021), https://www.cbinsights.com/research/startup-failure-post-mortem/.

46. Robert Fairlie and Sameeksha Desai, *2019 Early Stage Entrepreneurship* (Kaufman Indicators of Entrepreneurship, June 2020), https://indicators.kauffman.org/wp-content/uploads/sites/2/2020/05/2019_Early-Stage-Entrepreneurship-National-and-State-Report_final.pdf.

47. Steve Hawk, "Inside the Secret World of Venture Capital," *Stanford*

Graduate School of Business, June 20, 2018, https://www.gsb.stanford.edu/insights/inside-secret-world-venture-capital.

48. "Record Year for US Venture Capital Industry," NCVA Blog, March 25, 2021, https://nvca.org/pressreleases/record-year-for-u-s-venture-capital-industry-despite-pandemic-and-economic-downturn/.

49. Sequoia Capital in Silicon Valley has raised thirty funds, made more than 1500 investments, achieved at least 320 exits through acquisitions and IPOs, and built up Apple, Google, Oracle, and more during its fifty-year history. In China, Sequoia Capital has tallied up thirty-three funds, inked nearly 700 investments, racked up eighty-six IPOs and M&A deals within sixteen years, and funded online retailer JD.com, TikTok maker ByteDance, electric car maker NIO, and group-buying super app Meituan.

50. Investment in Pittsburgh's Technology Sector, Innovation Works, March 23, 2022, https://pub.ey.com/public/2022/2201/2201-3958601/pittsburgh-technology2021/index.html.

51. Investment in Pittsburgh's Technology Sector, Innovation Works, March 17, 2021, https://www.innovationworks.org/event/report-launch-investment-in-pittsburghs-technology-sector/.

52. Digital infrastructure startup Containership shut down, and a Hitachi subsidiary bought its intellectual property in 2020.

53. NVCA 2021 Yearbook, March 2021, https://nvca.org/wp-content/uploads/2021/03/NVCA-2021-Yearbook.pdf.

54. Even in Georgia, where the African American population makes up 33 percent of the total, funding for Black founders represents only 4.9 percent of the total statewide. Crunchbase Diversity Spotlight, Funding to Black & Latinx Founders, October 2020, https://about.crunchbase.com/2020-diversity-spotlight-report/.

55. 81 percent of venture firms don't have a Black investor. Among startup executives, 2.6 percent are Latinx and 2.1 percent are Blacks—a large gap from their share of the working age population. Collin West, Gopinath Sundaramurthy, and Marlon Nichols, "Deconstructing the Pipeline Myth and the Case for More Diverse Managers," Kauffman Fellows, February 4, 2020, https://www.kauffmanfellows.org/journal_posts/the-pipeline-myth-ethnicity-fund-managers.

56. "The State of Access to Capital for Entrepreneurs," Ewing Marion Kauffman Foundation, February 5, 2019, https://www.kauffman.org/wp-content/uploads/2019/12/capital_access_lab_exec_summary_FINAL.pdf.

57. Black-owned businesses start with almost three times less financial capital overall ($35,205) than white-owned businesses ($106,720). They

typically obtain only about $500 from venture capital and angel financing compared with more than $18,500 for white-owned business founders. Robert W. Fairlie, Alicia Robb, and David T. Robinson, *Black and White, Access to Capital Among Minority-Owned Startups* (National Bureau of Economic Research, November 2020), https://www.nber.org/system/files/working_papers/w28154/w28154.pdf.

58. Njera Perkins, "Here Are the World's Black Billionaires in 2021," *AFROTECH*, May 13, 2021, https://afrotech.com/black-billionaires-2021.

59. Peter Richman, "Notable Companies Founded by Black Entrepreneurs," *Stacker*, February 17, 2021, https://stacker.com/stories/3825/notable-companies-founded-black-entrepreneurs.

60. "Top 50 Women in Tech," *Forbes*, 2018 ranking, https://www.forbes.com/profile/joy-buolamwini/?list=top-tech-women-america&sh=48af330b358a.

61. *The 2018 State of Women-Owned Businesses Report* (American Express, August 2018), https://archive.mbda.gov/news/blog/2018/08/number-firms-owned-minority-women-has-grown-163-2007.html.

62. "All In: Female Founders and CEOs in the US VC Ecosystem," *PitchBook*, December 7, 2020, https://pitchbook.com/news/reports/2020-all-in-female-founders-and-ceos-in-the-us-vc-ecosystem.

63. Gordon Gee led the University of Colorado, Brown University, Vanderbilt University, and Ohio State University, and he returned to WVU in 2014 as president, https://www.wvexecutive.com/gordon-gee/.

64. WVU dean Reyes became provost and vice chancellor of academic affairs at the University of Illinois-Chicago in mid-August 2021 after six years as dean of its College of Business and Economics and a prior twelve years at the Sam M. Walton College of Business at the University of Arkansas. The new dean at the Chambers College is Joshua Hall, previously associate dean, department chair, and economics professor. Retired adjutant general Jim Hoyer takes over as VP of Start-up West Virginia.

65. William H. Frey, *Census 2020*, (Brookings Institute, April 26, 2021), https://www.brookings.edu/research/census-2020-data-release/.

66. West Virginia Economic Outlook, 2020–2024, West Virginia University, John Chambers College of Business and Economics, November 2019, https://researchrepository.wvu.edu/bureau_be/311/.

67. Haley Nicole Usenick, "The Heart of Appalachia Is on Life Support," *University of Pittsburgh Law Review*, Summer 2020, https://lawreview.law.pitt.edu/ojs/index.php/lawreview/article/view/783.

68. Mining employment nationally dropped from a high of 92,000 in 2011 to about 53,000 employees in 2019, US Energy Information

Administration, *Today in Energy*, December 11, 2019, https://www.eia.gov/todayinenergy/detail.php?id=42275.

69. Coal-mining jobs in central Appalachia dropped to 22,131. Coal, US Energy Information Administration, Annual Report 2019, https://www.eia.gov/coal/; https://www.eia.gov/coal/annual/pdf/acr.pdf; https://www.eia.gov/todayinenergy/detail.php?id=44536.

70. West Virginia Job Loss During the NAFTA-WTO Period, 1994–2018, citing Bureau of Labor Statistics, West Virginia Economy; https://www.citizen.org/wp-content/uploads/Manu-WV-2-Pager-2018.pdf.

71. Philip Bump, How the Economy of West Virginia Has Changed over the Past 25 Years, *Washington Post*, March 3, 2017, https://www.washingtonpost.com/news/politics/wp/2017/03/03/how-the-economy-of-west-virginia-has-changed-over-the-past-25-years/.

72. Katelynn Harris, "Beyond the Numbers," US Bureau of Labor Statistics, November 2020; Manufacturing accounts for 9 percent of non-farm jobs nationally, down from 22 percent in 1979; mining and logging comprise less than 1 percent of jobs in the US in 2019, and a decline of 263,000 workers from 1979 to 2019, https://www.bls.gov/opub/btn/volume-9/forty-years-of-falling-manufacturing-employment.htm.

73. The heart of the twelve-state Appalachian region—coal country and hillbilly lands—was hit the hardest by the coal mine shutdowns and the decline of tobacco growing and small family farms, with new jobs to be found only in lower-paying service and retail sectors. Central Appalachia, Rural Home.org, Housing Assistance Counsel, accessed October 8, 2020, http://www.ruralhome.org/storage/documents/appalov.pdf.

74. The greater Appalachia region faces a digital divide: lower levels of computer device access (84.2 percent), broadband subscriptions (75 percent), and mobile phone data plans (51 percent) compared with national rates. Appalachian Regional Commission, Data Snapshot, March 3, 2018, https://www.arc.gov/wp-content/uploads/2018/03/DataSnapshot-IncomeAndPovertyInAppalachia.pdf; https://www.arc.gov/wp-content/uploads/2019/05/DataSnapshot-EmploymentInAppalachia-1.pdf; https://www.arc.gov/wp-content/uploads/2020/07/DataSnapshot-ComputerAndBroadbandAccessInAppalachia.pdf.

75. National Center for Health Statistics, Center for Disease Control and Prevention, September 13, 2020, https://www.cdc.gov/nchs/nvss/vsrr/drug-overdose-data.htm.

76. West Virginia Economic Outlook, 2020–2024, West Virginia University, John Chambers College of Business and Economics, November 2019, https://researchrepository.wvu.edu/bureau_be/311/.

77. Quick Facts, Portsmouth, Ohio; US Census Bureau; April 1, 2020, https://www.census.gov/quickfacts/fact/table/portsmouthcityohio/RHI725220.

78. "Income and Poverty in the US," US Census Bureau, September 15, 2020, https://www.census.gov/library/publications/2020/demo/p60-270.html.

79. "New Boston Coke," Abandoned, accessed November 1, 2021, https://abandonedonline.net/location/new-boston-coke/.

80. Andrew Lee Feight, "Sole Choice & the Portsmouth Shoe Industry," https://sciotohistorical.org/items/show/44?tour=5&index=8.

81. "More than $15 billion in Opportunity Fund Equity at End of 2020," Novogradac, February 3, 2021, https://www.novoco.com/news/novogradac-report-more-15-billion-opportunity-fund-equity-end-2020.

82. "Understanding the Epidemic," Centers for Disease Control and Prevention, March 17, 2021, https://www.cdc.gov/opioids/basics/epidemic.html.

83. "Ohio Overdose Deaths on Rise Again," Harm Reduction Ohio, February 25, 2020, https://www.harmreductionohio.org/special-report-ohio-overdose-deaths-on-rise-again-exceed-4000-in-2019/.

84. Portsmouth Crime Rate Report (Ohio), data based on FBI Report of Offenses Known to Law Enforcement, as of 2015 and updated, https://www.cityrating.com/crime-statistics/ohio/portsmouth.html.

85. Michael Collins, "Is Manufacturing Losing Its Toolbox?" *IndustryWeek*, August 16, 2019, https://www.industryweek.com/supply-chain/article/22028096/is-us-manufacturing-losing-its-toolbox.

86. Additive Manufacturing Landscape Report 2020, May 26, 2020, https://amfg.ai/2020/05/26/the-additive-manufacturing-industry-landscape-2020-231-companies-driving-digital-manufacturing/.

87. $23.75 Billion Additive Manufacturing Market Analysis, 2020–2027, Research And Markets, August 2020, https://www.researchandmarkets.com/reports/5206602/additive-manufacturing-market-analysis-by.

88. Colin Yasukochi, "2021 Scoring Tech Talent," *CBRE*, July 12, 2021, https://www.cbre.us/research-and-reports/scoring-tech-talent-in-north-america-2021.

89. Analysis of data from the US Patents and Trademark Office, fiscal year 2021, November 2021, https://www.statista.com/statistics/256731/number-of-patent-grants-in-the-us-by-state/.

90. Thomas O'Shaughnessy, "Top 20 Cities for Young Home Buyers," *Clever*, August 3, 2021, https://listwithclever.com/research/top-cities-for-millennial-home-buyers/.

91. Kathleen Achtenberg, "This Just In: Small Businesses, Startups Prove Key to Jumpstarting Michigan's Economy," 2021 Detroit Entrepreneurial Ecosystem Report, Michigan Economic Development Corporation, June 28, 2021, https://www.michiganbusiness.org/press-releases/2021/06/tji-small-businesses-startups-key-to-jumpstarting-mi-economy/.

92. Dayton Opportunity Zones, July 9, 2019, https://dashboards.mysidewalk.com/dayton-oh-opportunity-zones-4d3d04b7182d/home-d8862dea349b.

93. US Department of Housing and Urban Development, New Report on Opportunity Zones, August 25, 2020, https://www.hud.gov/press/press_releases_media_advisories/HUD_No_20_131.

94. Gary Wagner, "Rust and Renewal," Federal Reserve Bank of Cleveland, February 2018, https://www.clevelandfed.org/region/industrial-heartland/retrospectives.aspx.

95. Branch has raised $82.5 million and was seeded by New York's Greycroft Partners. Two other insurers recently relocated to Columbus: Matic from Los Angeles, which picked up $24 million from IA Capital and Nationwide Ventures; and travel insurer Battleface, which banked $12 million from Drive Capital.

96. Cleveland Diagnostics took in $19.4 million led by Shanghai-based LYFE Capital to conduct tests for early detection of cancers. NeuroTherapia nabbed $8.8 million, led by San Francisco–based Brain Trust Accelerator Fund II to develop therapies for Alzheimer's disease. MediView XR came out of stealth in late 2017 with $4.5 million in funding from Plug and Play Ventures and two Ohio venture groups.

97. Checkpoint Surgical, a developer of a surgical device for nerve protection and repair, raised nearly $29 million, initially from JumpStart, and $8.8 million more in 2018, led by Mutual Capital Partners in Cleveland. Neuros Medical, a developer of an electrical nerve block to treat chronic pain, picked up $38.5 million in early 2021, adding to $20 million in 2017.

98. Roy Hansen, Hal Wolman, and David Connolly, "Finding a New Voice for Corporate Leaders in a Changed Urban World," George Washington Institute of Public Policy case study, (Brookings Institution, September 2006), https://www.brookings.edu/wp-content/uploads/2016/07/20060901_cleveland.pdf.

99. Michael Machosky, "How Pittsburgh Is Transforming into the Robotics Capital of the World," *Next Pittsburgh*, June 29, 2021; https://nextpittsburgh.com/city-design/how-pittsburgh-is-transforming-into-the-robotics-capital-of-the-world/.

100. 2021 Pittsburgh State of the Industry, Pittsburgh Technology Council,

September 20, 2021, https://www.pghtech.org/news and publications/
SOI_2021.

101. "Pittsburgh Tomorrow" (podcast), *Pittsburgh Quarterly*, September 16,
2020, https://pittsburghquarterly.com/articles/pittsburgh-tomorrow-
podcast-david-mawhinney-part-2/.

102. JumpStart News, May 13, 2021, https://www.jumpstartinc.org/
press/startups-and-small-businesses-generated-1b-in-economic-output-
across-ohio-in-2020/.

103. JobsOhio, Research and Innovation, Ohio Economic Development Organization, https://www.jobsohio.com/why-ohio/research-innovation/.

104. *Cleveland Plain Dealer*, editorial, June 9, 2019, https://www.
cleveland.com/opinion/2019/06/gov-dewine-and-lt-gov-husted-
should-prioritize-third-frontier-innovation-bond-renewal-editorial.
html.

105. Emily Fisher, "Venture Capital in Detroit Is Growing," *Detroit Is It*,
August 2, 2021, https://detroitisit.com/venture-capital-in-detroit-is-
growing/.

106. "Innovative Activity Overcomes Pandemic Disruption," World Intellectual Property Organization, February 10, 2022, https://www.wipo.
int/pressroom/en/articles/2022/article_0002.html.

107. "The State of US Science and Engineering 2022," National Science
Board, January 18, 2022, https://ncses.nsf.gov/pubs/nsb20221/
u-s-and-global-research-and-development.

108. NVCA 2022 Yearbook, March 2022, https://nvca.org/wp-content/
uploads/2022/03/NVCA-2022-Yearbook-Final.pdf.

109. "Global VC Funding Soars to $329.7 Billion," KPMG, January 19,
2022, https://assets.kpmg/content/dam/kpmg/xx/pdf/2022/01/
venture-pulse-q4-2021.pdf.

110. "$1B+ Market Map: The World's 1,066 Companies in One List," *CB
Insights*, March 29, 2022, https://www.cbinsights.com/research/
unicorn-startup-market-map/.

111. Rebecca A. Fannin, *Tech Titans of China* (New York: Hachette,
September 2019), https://www.amazon.com/Tech-Titans-China-
challenging-innovating/dp/1529374499.

112. Thilo Hanemann, Daniel H. Rosen, Mark Witzke, Steve Bennion, and
Emma Smith, *Two-Way Street: 2021 Update US-China Investment
Trend* (Rhodium Group, May 2021), https://rhg.com/wp-content/
uploads/2021/05/RHG_TWS-2021_Full-Report_Final.pdf.

113. Impact report 2021, Innovation Works, March 2022, https://www.
innovationworks.org/about/impact/.

Index

Index

About the Author

Rebecca A. Fannin is a journalist, author of three books, and a media entrepreneur who has covered global innovation for more than twenty years. She grew up in the Ohio heartland town of Lancaster, the daughter of a history professor and a kindergarten teacher. A graduate of Ohio University, she started out at the *Dayton Journal Herald* newspaper and missed a decades-long decline of steel mills and coal mines in Appalachia by heading to New York City and later Silicon Valley for her career.

After stints in a reporter's cubicle at Crain Communications in Manhattan and an editorial post at the dotcom magazine *Red Herring* in San Francisco, she ventured to Beijing and Shanghai, becoming one of the first American journalists to document China's entrepreneurial rise. Inspired by the tech founders she interviewed, she formed Silicon Dragon Ventures as her own media and events group for startups and investors, and—during COVID—added an online show featuring venture capitalists. She became a regular contributor to CNBC, and her articles appeared in *Harvard Business Review*, *Inc.*, *Fast Company*, and *Forbes*.

Rebecca's forward-looking books, *Silicon Dragon*, *Startup Asia*, and *Tech Titans of China*, launched her as a commentator and public speaker. A guest on BBC, Bloomberg, Fox News, and NPR, and a quoted expert in the *New York Times*, she also has spoken at the Brookings Institution, Asia Society, and many universities, including Harvard, Yale, and Oxford.

Silicon Heartland brings Rebecca back to her homeland to explore the Midwest's comeback from the Rust Belt and to discover the roots of her own journey.